Introduction

The background to the update of PET

The Preliminary English Test (PET) was originally introduced in response to a demand for an examination at a lower level than that of the First Certificate in English and one which would be at the Council of Europe Threshold level, as defined by van Ek and Trim.

As standard practice in Cambridge ESOL, examinations are periodically reviewed as part of the examination production process, to ensure that they remain fair, up-to-date and in line with customer expectations. The PET examination was last revised in 1994.

As part of the detailed and comprehensive review of the Preliminary English Test which began in 1999, stakeholders were canvassed for opinions on the examinations. Teachers, Students, Local Secretaries and Senior Team Leaders provided Cambridge ESOL with valuable feedback about all aspects of PET. Cambridge ESOL received very encouraging responses from stakeholders around the world, and as a consequence the changes included in the updated tests are minimal. The updated examination in the format in this test book begins in March 2004. All new materials have been extensively trialled and, as before, all materials that go into the live question papers have been pretested to ensure that they are suitable for the PET candidature and, in terms of difficulty, are at the appropriate level.

The following summarises the changes to the PET papers.

PET Reading/Writing

- Reading Part 1 (signs and notices) is three-option multiple-choice (instead of four-option) and samples a wider range of type of notice, to include short personal messages (such as emails and 'post-it' messages).
- In Writing Part 1, students are given the beginning and end of the sentence for their sentence transformation task. This focuses the task solely onto the correct identification of the target structure.
- Writing Part 2 is a guided writing task with a strong communicative purpose.
- In Writing Part 3 (extended writing), there will be a choice of task to reflect the types of writing that PET-level students are producing in the classroom.

PET Listening

- Parts 1 and 2 are now three-option multiple-choice (instead of four-option).

PET Speaking

- Part 1 is more Interlocutor-led, but still focuses on the same area of personal information.

The review process leading to the update of PET has been carefully considered and all new task types have been thoroughly trialled to ensure that the materials are relevant and fair to PET candidates.

The level of PET

Cambridge ESOL has developed a series of examinations which equate to the Council of Europe Common European Framework language levels. Within the levels, the Preliminary English Test is at Cambridge Level Two. This corresponds to the Council of Europe Level B1. This is shown in the chart below.

CAMBRIDGE / ALTE LEVELS   COUNCIL OF EUROPE LEVELS

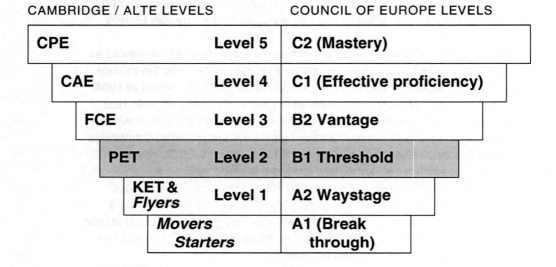

CAMBRIDGE / ALTE LEVELS		COUNCIL OF EUROPE LEVELS
CPE	Level 5	C2 (Mastery)
CAE	Level 4	C1 (Effective proficiency)
FCE	Level 3	B2 Vantage
PET	Level 2	B1 Threshold
KET & Flyers	Level 1	A2 Waystage
Movers Starters		A1 (Break through)

In the chart, the Main Suite examinations are shown in capitals (KET, PET, FCE, CAE and CPE) and the Young Learner examinations in italics.

Cambridge ESOL is a member of the Association of Language Testers in Europe (ALTE). The members are all providers of examinations in European languages, and one of their principal objectives is to establish a framework of levels of proficiency in order to promote the transnational recognition of certification.

Threshold

PET is based on the Council of Europe's Threshold document. This represents an intermediate level of language ability that should be attainable in about 375 hours according to Threshold.

The materials a Threshold user can deal with

The text types that can be handled by the learner at this level include street signs and public notices, product packaging, brochures, city guides and instructions on how to do things, as well as informal letters and newspaper and magazine texts, such as articles, features and weather forecasts. The kinds of listening texts the learner needs to understand are announcements made at railway stations and airports, traffic information given on the radio, public announcements made at sporting events or pop

Cambridge
Preliminary English Test
4

TEACHER'S BOOK

Examination papers from University of Cambridge ESOL Examinations: English for Speakers of Other Languages

CAMBRIDGE
UNIVERSITY PRESS

013960465 2

CAMBRIDGE UNIVERSITY PRESS
Cambridge, New York, Melbourne, Madrid, Cape Town,
Singapore, São Paulo, Delhi, Mexico City

Cambridge University Press
The Edinburgh Building, Cambridge CB2 8RU, UK

Published in the United States of America by Cambridge University Press, New York

www.cambridge.org
Information on this title: www.cambridge.org/9780521755290

First published 2003
3rd printing 2005

A catalogue record for this publication is available from the British Library

ISBN-13 978-0-521-75529-0 Teacher's Book
ISBN-13 978-0-521-75527-6 Student's Book
ISBN-13 978-0-521-75528-3 Student's Book with answers
ISBN-13 978-0-521-75530-6 Set of 2 Cassettes
ISBN-13 978-0-521-75531-3 Set of 2 Audio CDs
ISBN-13 978-0-521-75532-0 Self-study Pack

ISBN 978-0-521-75529-0 Paperback

Contents

concerts and instructions given by police or customs officials. At Threshold level, candidates need to be able not only to pick out facts, but also to understand opinions, attitudes, moods and wishes.

What a Threshold user can do

Learners at this level, if travelling as tourists, can get all the information needed from a tourist information centre, as long as it is of a straightforward, non-specialised nature. Similarly, if taking part in a guided tour, they can understand the main points of a commentary and ask questions in order to get more information, as long as no specialised technical language is needed. They can deal with most situations likely to arise when making travel arrangements through a travel agent or when actually travelling. In the context of work they can state requirements within their own job area, and ask questions of a fact-finding nature. In a meeting, they can take part in a discussion which involves the exchange of factual information or receiving instructions, but they may have difficulty dealing with anything unpredictable or unfamiliar. Where telephone calls are concerned, predictability is also important at this level, and as long as only routine matters are involved, the learner can receive and pass on messages. They can write simple personal letters within a more or less standard format.

Preparing for PET

Since PET is designed to test candidates' ability to perform language tasks similar to those required for successful performance in real life situations, practice in using English in realistic situations is the best way to prepare for PET.

Reading

Preparation is best done by giving students a wide variety of reading materials, including simple articles, reports, reviews, descriptions and narratives, particularly the type of English that is used in everyday life – advertisements, instructions and signs.

Practice should include extensive reading of texts as well as intensive reading, to give practice in skimming and scanning skills in order to understand the general meaning of a text or to look for specific information. For this, simplified readers are useful, also English language magazines in class libraries. Students should be encouraged to read widely about anything that interests them.

Writing

Practice should be given in short, controlled writing tasks, where the writing is for a specific, realistic purpose, for example, replies to letters, advertisements or invitations, diary entries, filling in forms, writing messages, including phone messages, writing short notes and letters to friends. Keeping a diary in English and writing to penfriends are particularly useful forms of practice for students.

Letter-writing is a very important skill which requires regular practice. Letter-writing layout is not tested, but candidates are expected to recognise and use appropriate salutations and endings. Letters to a friend relating to past experiences, present activities and future plans are likely to provide helpful practice.

It is just as important to attend to meaning as it is to attend to forms of language. In the exam, errors which do not hinder communication are not penalised as heavily as errors which cause a breakdown in communication.

Listening

Students should be encouraged to listen to as many different sources of English as they can, for example, films, television, radio and airport announcements; they may also be able to hear English spoken in hotels, shops, restaurants, at the British Council, by tourist guides, etc. Listening to native speakers or fairly fluent non-native speakers is the best practice they can get.

Teachers can also collect recordings of short talks and conversations as well as using published language-teaching cassettes and videos. When devising practice material, teachers should remember that candidates will not normally be required to recall particular words used, but rather to understand and remember the meaning of a listening passage.

Speaking

Students should practise eliciting and giving simple information about themselves, for example, their name and its spelling, where they live, what they do, their interests, likes and dislikes.

It would be very helpful for students to do this by spending time regularly talking to a friend in English about what they have been doing and about their plans, etc.

In class, simple role-plays can provide an opportunity for spontaneous speech, but it is important that students are able to recognise and relate to the roles and that they are given a specific, purposeful task.

Students should always be encouraged to give reasons to justify the opinions or views they put forward.

PET candidates

Information is collected about the PET candidates at each session of the examination when candidates complete a Candidate Information Sheet.

In 2002, there were approximately 100,000 candidates for PET throughout the world. The candidates for PET come from a wide range of backgrounds and take the examination for a number of different reasons. The candidate profile for PET in terms of age, educational background and employment/studies varies according to geophysical regions. The design of questions in PET takes into account the potential diversity of age and linguistic/cultural background of candidates. The following points summarise the characteristics of the current PET candidature:

Nationality

PET is taken by candidates in more than 80 countries. The majority of these candidates enter for PET in European and South American countries. Many candidates take the examination in the UK, and significant numbers take the test in the Middle East and Far East.

Age and gender

The majority of candidates are in the 14–18 age group (52%). A further 22% are in the 19–25 age group; 14% of candidates are aged 13 and under and 12% are 26 and over. About 55% of candidates are female.

Employment

Most candidates (about 70%) are in full-time education.

Exam preparation

A large proportion of candidates (about 85%) undertake a preparatory course before taking the examination.

Reasons for taking PET

Candidates' reasons for wanting an English language qualification at PET level are shown below:
- to gain employment (33%)
- for further study (31%)
- out of personal interest (36%)

Further information

PET is held each year in March, May, June (twice), November and December in centres around the world.

Current information on dates and the administrative details of the examination are provided separately to centres. A copy can be obtained from your nearest Cambridge ESOL Examination Centre. A list of Cambridge ESOL Examination Centres is obtainable from Cambridge ESOL (address below) or from the website (address below). All PET entries must be made through an authorised Centre.

Further information can be obtained from:

The Cambridge ESOL Helpdesk
University of Cambridge ESOL Examinations
1 Hills Road
Cambridge
CB1 2EU
United Kingdom
Tel: +44 1223 553997   Fax: +44 1223 460278
Email: ESOLHelpdesk@UCLES.org.uk
Website www.CambridgeESOL.org

In some areas this information can also be obtained from the British Council.

PET content and marking

Candidates record their answers in pencil on a separate OMR (Optical Mark Reader) answer sheet for the Reading/Writing and Listening papers. The answer sheets are then scanned by computer. Writing Parts 1 and 2 and Listening Part 3 are double marked by a team of fully trained markers who are closely supervised at every stage. The assessment and marking of Writing Part 3 and the Speaking test are described in detail later in this section.

The OMR answer sheets are given out with Paper 1 (Reading and Writing) and no extra time is allowed for candidates to transfer answers from their question paper to the answer sheet.

For the Listening component, candidates should make a note of their answers on the question paper. They are then given extra time to transfer these answers to the OMR answer sheet at the end of the test.

Examples of the OMR answer sheets are given at the back of the Student's Book.

PET consists of three papers:

Paper 1	1 hour 30 mins	Reading	5 parts	25%
		Writing	3 parts	25%
Paper 2	35 mins including 6 mins transfer time	Listening	4 parts	25%
Paper 3	10–12 mins	Speaking	4 parts	25%

Paper 1   Reading and Writing (1 hour 30 minutes)

In the PET Reading and Writing Paper, five parts focus on reading and three parts focus on writing.

READING

Part	Text type	Focus	Task	Marks
1	Signs, notices, messages, emails and other very short texts found in common contexts in everyday life	Reading for main message and some detail	5 multiple-choice questions, each with 3 options	5
2	Brief descriptions of 5 people and a set of 8 factual texts with a common theme, e.g. extracts from holiday brochures, book reviews, film guides, descriptions of consumer goods	Reading for detailed understanding	Matching each of 5 descriptions of people and their needs to one of the 8 texts	5

Part	Text type	Focus	Task	Marks
3	A factual text, e.g. a public notice, advice leaflet, consumer information, advert, excerpt from a brochure, etc.	Scanning for specific information	10 true/false questions	10
4	A text which conveys an attitude or opinion as well as factual information, e.g. a newspaper article, review, letter, etc.	Reading to understand writer's purpose and attitude or opinion Reading for global and detailed meaning	5 multiple-choice questions, each with 4 options	5
5	A factual or narrative text, e.g. a newspaper report or magazine article, with gaps	Reading for global and detailed meaning Identifying the appropriate lexical or structural item	10 multiple-choice cloze questions, each with 4 options	10

The type of text varies according to the different test focus of each part. Texts are authentic, but may have been edited to bring vocabulary and structure within the grasp of students at this level. Texts may contain occasional vocabulary items or structures unfamiliar to many candidates at this level, but they will be able to deduce the meaning from the context, and understanding of these words will not be necessary to complete the task.

Part 1

Candidates look at five notices, signs, messages, etc. each containing a short text. A multiple-choice question tests their understanding of each. Candidates should be able to deduce the purpose of the notice, and understand its meaning, but they do not need to understand every word.

Part 2

This tests detailed comprehension of factual material. Candidates read a short description of five people and their needs and have to match each person to one of eight short, factual texts which typically give information about places, products, services, entertainments, etc. Three of the texts will either not match at all, or will only partially fit.

Part 3

This tests a candidate's ability to scan a fairly lengthy text (about 400 words) to search for specific information in order to answer ten true/false questions. There will be redundant information in the text and candidates may meet vocabulary which is not familiar to them. However, they will not need to understand such vocabulary in order to answer the questions, and if they meet an unfamiliar word they should be encouraged to read on and concentrate on finding the information asked for.

Part 4

This text goes beyond the provision of factual information and expresses an attitude or opinion. Candidates are required to read the text very carefully to answer the multiple-choice questions which may test whether they have understood the writer's purpose in writing the text and the attitude expressed in the text, as well as whether they have understood the meaning of the text as a whole.

Part 5

Candidates read a short text containing ten numbered gaps. There is a multiple-choice question for each gap at the end of the passage. The text is usually an extract from a newspaper, magazine or story and the questions are designed to test vocabulary and grammatical points.

   Candidates should be encouraged to read the whole text before answering the questions and be reminded that they will need to read the complete sentence before they can decide which option fits.

Marks

The 35 marks for this component are weighted to give a total of 25 marks, i.e. 25% of the marks available for the whole test.

WRITING

Part	Focus	Task	Marks
1	Sentence transformation	5 sentences to rewrite	5
2	Communicative writing	Continuous writing of 35–45 words	5
3	Letter-writing or story-writing	Continuous writing of about 100 words	15

Part 1

This is a grammar transformation task. Candidates are given a sentence and then asked to complete another version of it using a different structural pattern but so that it still has the same meaning. They are given the beginning and end of the sentence and they have to complete the middle part. There may be more than one correct answer in some cases. There are five questions plus a worked example, and all the sentences are theme-related.

Part 2

This is a short communicative piece of writing (35–45 words). Students need to transmit three pieces of information. The rubric or input text informs students what they need to communicate to the reader.

Part 3

In this part, candidates are required to write an informal letter or story of about 100 words.

Marks

There is a total of 25 marks in the writing component, which translates to 25% of the marks available for the whole test.

Assessment of Writing Part 2

The focus of Part 2 is on addressing the three content points. The General Mark scheme below is used in conjunction with a Task-specific Mark scheme (see Test keys).

Writing Part 2: General Mark scheme	
5	All content elements covered appropriately. Message clearly communicated to reader.
4	All content elements adequately dealt with. Message communicated successfully, on the whole.
3	All content elements attempted. Message requires some effort by the reader. OR One content element omitted but others clearly communicated.
2	Two content elements omitted, or unsuccessfully dealt with. Message only partly communicated to reader. OR Script may be slightly short (20–25 words).
1	Little relevant content and/or message requires excessive effort by the reader, or short (10–19 words).
0	Totally irrelevant or totally incomprehensible or too short (under 10 words).

Assessment of Writing Part 3

Candidates are expected to write a coherent letter or story in an appropriately informal style. Credit is given for reasonably correct grammar, spelling and punctuation and appropriate use of a range of vocabulary. Candidates are expected to show a clear ending to their letter. They will be penalised if they write too few words (less than 80). They will not be penalised if they write too much, but they are advised not to do so, as there is only a limited amount of writing space on the answer sheet.

Candidates' continuous writing is assessed according to the criteria below. Note that there are different levels of performance within each Band which translate to a mark out of 15.

This Mark scheme is provided for each examiner, along with a set of sample scripts which are chosen to demonstrate the range of responses and different levels of competence achieved in this writing task. This therefore provides a common standard of assessment for all examiners to use. Standardisation takes place before marking commences and all examiners are monitored during the marking exercise to ensure consistent standards and reliability of marking.

Note: This Mark scheme is **interpreted at PET level.**

Writing Part 3: General Mark scheme	
Band 5	**Very good attempt:** • Confident and ambitious use of language • Wide range of structures and vocabulary within the task set • Well organised and coherent, through use of simple linking devices • Errors are minor, due to ambition and non-impeding Requires no effort by the reader
Band 4	**Good attempt:** • Fairly ambitious use of language • More than adequate range of structures and vocabulary within the task set • Evidence of organisation and some linking of sentences • Some errors, generally non-impeding Requires only a little effort by the reader
Band 3	**Adequate attempt:** • Language is unambitious, or if ambitious, flawed • Adequate range of structures and vocabulary • Some attempt at organisation; linking of sentences not always maintained • A number of errors may be present, but are mostly non-impeding Requires some effort by the reader
Band 2	**Inadequate attempt:** • Language is simplistic/limited/repetitive • Inadequate range of structures and vocabulary • Some incoherence; erratic punctuation • Numerous errors, which sometimes impede communication Requires considerable effort by the reader

Band 1	**Poor attempt:** • Severely restricted command of language • No evidence of range of structures and vocabulary • Seriously incoherent; absence of punctuation • Very poor control; difficult to understand Requires excessive effort by the reader	
Band 0	**Achieves nothing:** Language impossible to understand, or totally irrelevant to task	

Paper 2   Listening (about 35 minutes including 6 minutes transfer time)

The PET Listening Paper is divided into four parts with a total of 25 questions.

The listening passages are recorded on cassette and CD and each is heard twice. The speed of delivery is at the slower end of the range of a normal speaking speed. There are pauses for the candidates to check their answers. The instructions to the candidates on the cassette/CD mirror the instructions on the question paper. Candidates put their answers on the question paper as they listen, and they are then given six minutes at the end of the test to transfer these answers to an answer sheet.

The listening material is written or adapted specifically for the test and recorded in a studio to simulate real spoken language.

Part	Type of recording	Focus	Task	Marks
1	7 separate short dialogues or monologues in neutral or informal contexts	Listening for detailed meaning and specific information	7 multiple-choice questions (pictorial), each with 3 options	7
2	A semi-formal prompted monologue or interview, e.g. radio interview, factual announcement, recorded message	Listening for detailed meaning, distinguishing between main and secondary points	6 multiple-choice questions, each with 3 options	6
3	A semi-formal or prompted monologue, e.g. radio report, narrative account, recorded message	Listening to identify specific information Listening and writing down information	6 gaps to fill	6
4	A dialogue	Listening for global and detailed meaning Listening to identify speakers' attitudes and feelings	6 yes/no questions	6

Part 1

Candidates hear seven short monologues and dialogues, each accompanied by a question and three illustrations, and they have to put a tick below the picture which answers the question.

Part 2

The recording for this contains information which may be of interest to candidates without concerning them directly, e.g. news or current affairs broadcasts, a simple narrative relating an incident or an account of future events, plans or programmes. It is more likely to contain redundant material than other parts. Candidates have to answer six multiple-choice questions which test understanding of either specific information or clearly stated attitude or opinion.

Part 3

This is a recording containing factual information of the kind candidates may need or want, such as information about travel, the weather, opening times, facilities available, etc. Candidates have to extract specific information in order to fill in six gaps on a form or a set of notes, which requires them to write one, two or three words, or numbers, dates, etc.

Part 4

Candidates listen to a conversation between two people in which they express opinions, agree or disagree, etc. as well as exchanging information. Candidates have to answer six yes/no questions which test their understanding of opinions and attitudes, as well as their understanding of the gist of the conversation.

Marks

One mark is given for each correct answer, making a possible total of 25 marks, which makes up 25% of the marks available for the whole test.

Paper 3 Speaking (10–12 minutes)

The PET Speaking test is conducted by two examiners (an Interlocutor and an Assessor) with pairs of candidates. The Assessor takes no part in the interaction. It takes 10–12 minutes for each pair of candidates. Where there is an odd number of candidates at an examining session, the last test will be for a group of three candidates. In this case, the test will last 13–15 minutes. The Speaking test is divided into four parts.

Part	Focus	Skills	Time
1	Giving personal information	Socialising, interacting and giving personal information	2–3 mins
2	Simulated situation	Expressing and finding out attitudes, discussing alternatives, agreeing/disagreeing, making choices	2–3 mins
3	Describing a photograph	Giving information, describing, structuring discourse, comparing and contrasting, paraphrasing	3 mins
4	General conversation based on theme from Part 3	Giving and obtaining factual information, expressing and finding out opinions and attitudes, structuring discourse, socialising	3 mins

Part 1

In this part, candidates interact with the Interlocutor, using the language normally associated with meeting people for the first time. Candidates are asked to talk about, for example, their home town, school, occupation, family, interests, etc.

Part 2

In this part, the two candidates interact with each other. The Interlocutor describes a situation to the candidates, in response to which they are required to make suggestions, discuss alternatives, state preferences, etc. Candidates are given a visual prompt to help stimulate ideas for their discussion.

Part 3

In this part, each candidate in turn is given a colour photograph to talk about. Candidates should be encouraged to talk about the setting, people and activities. Specialised vocabulary is not expected at PET level, but candidates should be able to paraphrase. The two photographs are linked thematically to establish a common starting point for Part 4.

Part 4

In this part, the theme of the photographs in Part 3 (for example, holiday activities) is used as a starting point for a general conversation about the candidates' likes and dislikes, experiences and habits. The Interlocutor initiates the discussion but the candidates are expected to talk between themselves. They should be able to talk about their interests and reasons for liking or not liking something. The Interlocutor will use prompts if the discussion fails to develop.

Assessment and marking

Throughout the Speaking test candidates are assessed on their language skills, not their personality, intelligence or knowledge of the world. Candidates at this level are not expected to be fully fluent or accurate speakers, but they are expected to be able to interact appropriately, develop the conversation and respond to the tasks set.

The language of the Speaking test is carefully controlled to be accessible to candidates at this level; if candidates do not understand a question or an instruction they should ask for repetition or clarification and they will normally get credit for using this strategy. Similarly, they will get credit for using paraphrase to supplement any inadequate linguistic resources.

Candidates are assessed on their own individual performance according to established criteria and are not assessed in relation to each other. Where candidates are required to interact with each other, they will get credit for cooperating to negotiate meaning, but one candidate will not be penalised for another's shortcomings.

The score on the Speaking test is weighted to 25% of the marks for the whole test. The marks given are awarded on the basis of the following criteria: Grammar and Vocabulary, Discourse Management, Pronunciation and Interactive Communication.

Grammar and Vocabulary

This scale refers to the accurate and appropriate use of grammatical forms and vocabulary. It also includes the range of both grammatical forms and vocabulary. Performance is viewed in terms of the overall effectiveness of the language used in dealing with the tasks.

Discourse Management

This scale refers to the coherence, extent and relevance of each candidate's individual contribution. On this scale the candidate's ability to maintain a coherent flow of language is assessed, either within a single utterance or over a string of utterances. Also assessed here is how relevant the contributions are to what has gone before.

Pronunciation

This scale refers to the candidate's ability to produce comprehensible utterances to fulfil the task requirements. This includes stress, rhythm and intonation, as well as individual sounds. Examiners put themselves in the position of the non-language specialist and assess the overall impact of the pronunciation and the degree of effort required to understand the candidate. Different varieties of English, e.g. British, North American, Australian etc., are acceptable, provided they are used consistently throughout the test.

Interactive Communication

This scale refers to the candidate's ability to use language to achieve meaningful communication. This includes initiating and responding without undue hesitation, the ability to use interactive strategies to maintain or repair communication, and sensitivity to the norms of turn-taking.

Standardisation

All Oral Examiners are fully trained, so that they conduct the Speaking test and award marks in a standardised way. In countries where the Cambridge ESOL Team Leader system is in place, standardisation of procedure and assessment is maintained both by attendance at regular coordination sessions and by monitoring visits to centres by Team Leaders. In countries outside the Team Leader system, experienced Oral Examiners run training and standardisation/coordination sessions for Local Examiners, using materials provided by Cambridge ESOL.

Grading, awards and results

Grading

Grading takes place once all answer sheets and mark sheets have been returned to Cambridge ESOL and marking is complete. This is approximately four weeks after the examination.

The final grade boundaries are set using the following information:

- information on the difficulty level of individual items and the components as a whole (from Pretesting information and the use of anchor tests)
- data on the candidates
- data on the overall candidate performance
- statistics on individual items, for those parts of the examination for which this is appropriate (Papers 1 and 2)

A candidate's overall PET grade is based on the aggregate score gained by the candidate across all three papers.

Grade Review takes place immediately after Grading. All candidates who have failed the examination by a very small margin have their Writing Component mark checked.

Special Circumstances

Special Circumstances covers three main areas: Special Arrangements, Special Consideration and Malpractice.

Special Arrangements: these are available for candidates with a long-term disability such as hearing/sight impairment, dyslexia or a speech impediment, or short-term difficulties such as a broken arm. They may include extra time, separate accommodation or equipment, Braille transcription, etc. Consult the Cambridge ESOL Local Secretary in your area for more details.

Special Consideration: Cambridge ESOL may give Special Consideration to candidates affected by adverse circumstances immediately before or during an examination. Applications for Special Consideration are submitted by centres and must be made within two weeks of the examination date.

Malpractice: the Malpractice Committee will consider cases where candidates are suspected of copying or collusion, or where other breaches of exam regulations are reported. Results may be withheld pending further investigation. Centres are notified if a candidate is suspected of malpractice.

Results

Statements of Results are usually sent out about five or six weeks after the date of the examination. Results are reported in the following way: there are two pass grades ('Pass with Merit' and 'Pass'), and two fail grades ('Narrow Fail' and 'Fail').

Pass with Merit ordinarily corresponds to a mark of 85% and above in the examination. Pass usually represents a mark of between 70 and 85%. A Narrow Fail result indicates that the candidate was within 5% of the Pass boundary.

Each candidate is provided with a Statement of Results which includes a graphical display of the candidate's performance in each paper. These are shown against the scale Exceptional – Good – Borderline – Weak and indicate the candidate's relative performance in each paper.

Certificates are sent to candidates achieving one of the pass grades within six weeks of the despatch of Statements of Results.

Frames for the Speaking test

The pictures referred to here are in the Colour Section in the centre of the Student's Book (pages I–VIII).

TEST 1

PART 1   GENERAL CONVERSATION

Tasks	Identifying oneself; giving information about oneself; talking about interests.
Sub-tasks	Spelling; responding to questions.
Framework	*In this section the examiner asks questions in order to elicit information about personal details, home town, schools, jobs, family, etc.*
	The task requires the students to respond to the examiner's questions.
Time	2–3 minutes.

PART 2   SIMULATED SITUATION (SEA-SIDE TOWN)

Tasks	Discussing alternatives; expressing opinions; making choices.
Framework	*Say (slowly) to both students:*

> 'I'm going to describe a situation to you.
>
> A small sea-side town wants more tourists to visit all year round. Talk together about the different things the town could build for tourists and say which would be best.
>
> Here is a picture with some ideas to help you.'

Ask both students to look at picture 1A on page I of the Student's Book and repeat the frame.

> 'I'll say that again.
>
> A small sea-side town wants more tourists to visit all year round. Talk together about the different things the town could build for tourists and say which would be best.
>
> All right? Talk together.'

Allow the students enough time to complete the task without intervention. Prompt only if necessary.

The task requires the students to arrive at a conclusion without prompting.

Time	2–3 minutes (including time to assimilate the information).

PART 3   DESCRIBING A PHOTOGRAPH (LEARNING A SKILL)

Tasks   Describing people and places; saying where people and things are and what different people are doing.

Framework   *Say to both students:*

> 'Now, I'd like each of you to talk on your own about something. I'm going to give each of you a photograph of some people learning a skill.
>
> Student A, here is your photograph. (*Ask Student A to look at photo 1B on page II of the Student's Book.*) Please show it to Student B, but I'd like you to talk about it. Student B, you just listen. I'll give you your photograph in a moment.
>
> Student A, please tell us what you can see in your photograph. Thank you.'

If there is a need to intervene, prompts rather than direct questions should be used.

Ask Student A to close his/her book.

> 'Now, Student B, here is your photograph. It also shows people learning a skill. (*Ask Student B to look at photo 1C on page IV of the Student's Book.*) Please show it to Student A and tell us what you can see in your photograph. Thank you.'

The students should talk about the photographs with little or no prompting. They are not expected to use specialised words, but the ability to paraphrase is expected if required.

Ask the students to close their books before moving to Part 4.

PART 4   GENERAL CONVERSATION BASED ON THE PHOTOGRAPHS

Tasks   Talking about one's likes and dislikes; expressing opinions.

Framework   *Say to both students:*

> 'Your photographs showed people learning a skill. Now, I'd like you to talk to each other about the skills you would like to learn and how they would be useful.'

Allow the students enough time to complete the task without intervention. Prompt only if necessary.

The task is achieved if the students can talk about the skills they would like to learn, and how they would be useful, with little or no prompting.

Time   **Parts 3 and 4** should take about **6 minutes** together.

TEST 2

PART 1   GENERAL CONVERSATION

Tasks   Identifying oneself; giving information about oneself; talking about interests.

Sub-tasks   Spelling; responding to questions.

Framework   *In this section the examiner asks questions in order to elicit information about personal details, home town, schools, jobs, family, etc.*

The task requires the students to respond to the examiner's questions.

Time   2–3 minutes.

PART 2   SIMULATED SITUATION (TRIP TO ENGLAND)

Tasks   Discussing alternatives; expressing opinions; making choices.

Framework   *Say (slowly) to both students:*

> 'I'm going to describe a situation to you.
>
> A friend of yours is planning to spend 6 months in England to improve her English. Talk together about the things she will need in England, and decide which are the most important things to take/bring with her.
>
> Here is a picture with some ideas to help you.'

Ask both students to look at picture 2A on page III of the Student's Book and repeat the frame.

> 'I'll say that again.
>
> A friend of yours is planning to spend 6 months in England to improve her English. Talk together about the things she will need in England, and decide which are the most important things to take/bring with her.
>
> All right? Talk together.'

Allow the students enough time to complete the task without intervention. Prompt only if necessary.

The task requires the students to arrive at a conclusion without prompting.

Time 2–3 minutes (including time to assimilate the information).

PART 3 DESCRIBING A PHOTOGRAPH (LETTERS)

Tasks Describing people and places; saying where people and things are and what different people are doing.

Framework *Say to both students:*

> 'Now, I'd like each of you to talk on your own about something. I'm going to give each of you a photograph of people with letters.
>
> Student A, here is your photograph. (*Ask Student A to look at photo 2B on page IV of the Student's Book.*) Please show it to Student B but I'd like you to talk about it. Student B, you just listen. I'll give you your photograph in a moment.
>
> Student A, please tell us what you can see in your photograph. Thank you.'

If there is a need to intervene, prompts rather than direct questions should be used.

Ask Student A to close his/her book.

> 'Now, Student B, here is your photograph. It also shows someone with a letter. (*Ask Student B to look at photo 2C on page II of the Student's Book.*) Please show it to Student A and tell us what you can see in your photograph.
>
> Thank you.'

The students should talk about the photographs with little or no prompting. They are not expected to use specialised words, but the ability to paraphrase is expected if required.

Ask the students to close their books before moving to Part 4.

PART 4 GENERAL CONVERSATION BASED ON THE PHOTOGRAPHS

Tasks Talking about one's likes and dislikes; expressing opinions.

Framework *Say to both students:*

> 'Your photographs showed people with letters. Now, I'd like you to talk together about the type of letters you like to write or receive, and other ways you keep in contact with people.'

Allow the students enough time to complete the task without intervention. Prompt only if necessary.

The task is achieved if the students can talk about the type of letters they like to write or receive, and other ways they keep in contact with people, with little or no prompting.

Time　　　　**Parts 3 and 4** should take about **6 minutes** together.

TEST 3

PART 1　GENERAL CONVERSATION

Tasks　　　Identifying oneself; giving information about oneself; talking about interests.

Sub-tasks　Spelling; responding to questions.

Framework　*In this section the examiner asks questions in order to elicit information about personal details, home town, schools, jobs, family, etc.*

The task requires the students to respond to the examiner's questions.

Time　　　　2–3 minutes.

PART 2　SIMULATED SITUATION (A LONG WAIT)

Tasks　　　Discussing alternatives; expressing opinions; making choices.

Framework　*Say (slowly) to both students:*

> 'I'm going to describe a situation to you.
>
> You are on a long car journey with some friends. The car breaks down in a small city. It will take three hours to repair it. Talk together about the different things you can do while you wait and decide which is best.
>
> Here is a picture with some ideas to help you.'

Ask both students to look at picture 3A on page V of the Student's Book and repeat the frame.

> 'I'll say that again.
>
> You are on a long car journey with some friends. The car breaks down in a small city. It will take three hours to repair it. Talk together about the different things you can do while you wait and decide which is best.
>
> All right? Talk together.'

Allow the students enough time to complete the task without intervention. Prompt only if necessary.

The task requires the students to arrive at a conclusion without prompting.

Time 2–3 minutes (including time to assimilate the information).

PART 3   DESCRIBING A PHOTOGRAPH (PLAYING GAMES)

Tasks Describing people and places; saying where people and things are and what different people are doing.

Framework *Say to both students:*

> 'Now, I'd like each of you to talk on your own about something. I'm going to give each of you a photograph of people playing games.
>
> Student A, here is your photograph. (*Ask Student A to look at photo 3B on page VI of the Student's Book.*) Please show it to Student B, but I'd like you to talk about it. Student B, you just listen. I'll give you your photograph in a moment.
>
> Student A, please tell us what you can see in your photograph. Thank you.'

If there is a need to intervene, prompts rather than direct questions should be used.

Ask Student A to close his/her book.

> 'Now, Student B, here is your photograph. It also shows someone playing games. (*Ask Student B to look at photo 3C on page VIII of the Student's Book.*) Please show it to Student A and tell us what you can see in your photograph.
>
> Thank you.'

The students should talk about the photographs with little or no prompting. They are not expected to use specialised words, but the ability to paraphrase is expected if required.

Ask the students to close their books before moving to Part 4.

PART 4   GENERAL CONVERSATION BASED ON THE PHOTOGRAPHS

Tasks   Talking about one's likes and dislikes; expressing opinions.

Framework   *Say to both students:*

> 'Your photographs showed people playing games. Now, I'd like you to talk together about the games you played when you were younger, and the games you like to play now.'

Allow the students enough time to complete the task without intervention. Prompt only if necessary.

The task is achieved if the students can talk about the games they played when they were younger, and the games they like to play now, with little or no prompting.

Time   **Parts 3 and 4** should take about **6 minutes** together.

TEST 4

PART 1   GENERAL CONVERSATION

Tasks   Identifying oneself; giving information about oneself; talking about interests.

Sub-tasks   Spelling; responding to questions.

Framework   *In this section the examiner asks questions in order to elicit information about personal details, home town, schools, jobs, family, etc.*

The task requires the students to respond to the examiner's questions.

Time   2–3 minutes.

PART 2   SIMULATED SITUATION (SUMMER ACTIVITIES)

Tasks   Discussing alternatives; expressing opinions; making choices.

Suitable for pairs or groups of three.

Framework   *Say (slowly) to both/all students:*

> 'I'm going to describe a situation to you.
>
> A sports club in your area is organising some summer activities for teenagers. Talk together about the kinds of sport teenagers enjoy and say which you think will be the most popular.
>
> Here is a picture with some ideas to help you.'

Ask both/all students to look at picture 4A on page VII of the Student's Book and repeat the frame.

> 'I'll say that again.
>
> A sports club in your area is organising some summer activities for teenagers. Talk together about the kinds of sport teenagers enjoy and say which you think will be the most popular.
>
> All right? Talk together.'

Allow the students enough time to complete the task without intervention. Prompt only if necessary.

The task requires the students to arrive at a conclusion without prompting.

Time   2–3 minutes for paired students and about 3 minutes for groups of three students (including time to assimilate the information).

PART 3   DESCRIBING A PHOTOGRAPH (TYPES OF MEALS)

Tasks   Describing people and places; saying where people and things are and what different people are doing.

Framework   *Say to both/all students:*

> 'Now, I'd like each of you to talk on your own about something. I'm going to give each of you a photograph of some people eating a meal.
>
> Student A, here is your photograph. (*Ask Student A to look at photo 4B on page VIII of the Student's Book.*) Please show it to Students B and C, but I'd like you to talk about it. Students B and C, you just listen. I'll give you your photographs in a moment.
>
> Student A, please tell us what you can see in your photograph. Thank you.'

If there is a need to intervene, prompts rather than direct questions should be used.

Ask Student A to close his/her book.

> 'Now, Student B, here is your photograph. It also shows people eating a meal. (*Ask Student B to look at photo 4C on page VI of the Student's Book.*) Please show it to Students A and C and tell us what you can see in your photograph. Thank you.'

Ask Student B to close his/her book.

'Now, Student C, here is your photograph. It also shows people eating a meal. (*Ask Student C to look at photo 4D on page VIII of the Student's Book.*) Please show it to Students A and B and tell us what you can see in your photograph.

Thank you.'

The students should talk about the photographs with little or no prompting. They are not expected to use specialised words, but the ability to paraphrase is expected if required.

Ask the students to close their books before moving to Part 4.

PART 4   GENERAL CONVERSATION BASED ON THE PHOTOGRAPHS

Tasks   Talking about one's likes and dislikes; expressing opinions.

Framework   *Say to both/all students:*

'Your photographs showed people eating a meal. Now, I'd like you to talk together about the kinds of meals you like to eat, and the kinds of meals you don't like.'

Allow the students enough time to complete the task without intervention. Prompt only if necessary.

The task is achieved if the students can talk about the kinds of meals they like to eat, and the kinds of meals they don't like, with little or no prompting.

Time   **Parts 3 and 4** should take about **6 minutes** together for paired students and **7–8 minutes** together for groups of three students.

Key

Test 1

READING

Part 1

1 A   2 C   3 B   4 A   5 C

Part 2

6 D   7 B   8 G   9 H   10 E

Part 3

11 B   12 B   13 A   14 A   15 A   16 B   17 A

18 B   19 A   20 A

Part 4

21 C   22 D   23 B   24 C   25 B

Part 5

26 B   27 C   28 D   29 B   30 A   31 C   32 B

33 D   34 C   35 A

WRITING

Part 1

1 My friend told me that I could stay in his flat.

| **My friend said: 'You** | can stay in/at | **my flat.'** |

2 I started living here two months ago.

| **I have lived here** | since | **two months ago.** |

3 This is the first time I've lived in a city.

| **I've** | never lived | **in a city before.** |

4 The flat has two bedrooms.

There	are two/2 bedrooms	**in the flat.**

5 My bedroom is too small for all my books.

My bedroom is not	large/big enough	**for all my books.**

Part 2

The Task-specific Mark scheme given below should be used in conjunction with the General Mark scheme for **Writing Part 2** given on page 13.

Task-specific Mark scheme

The content elements that need to be covered are:

i   which club you have joined
ii   a suggestion that Max should join the club
iii what you can do there together

The following sample answers can be used as a guide when marking.

SAMPLE A (Test 1, Question 6: Email to Max)

Hello Max
I am writing to you to ask that you can join our club.
This club is for make some foreign friends. I know that
you want to learn French and you don't have any
French friends. I want to learn French as well. If you join
us you can learn French with me. I will waiting for your
reply, bye.

Examiner Comments

All three content elements are covered appropriately and the message is clearly communicated. Candidates are not expected to include email format to get a 5.

Band: 5

SAMPLE B (Test 1, Question 6: Email to Max)

> Hope your doing well, and I'm well too, I'm just want to inform you, I'm joined in club which it called "Blue Club" which is in Barking, so I like you to come this weekend. We are going to play pool, dancing, drinking and many more.

Examiner Comments

In this script, all three content elements are covered and the message is communicated successfully on the whole, although the language errors require some effort by the reader.

Band: 4

SAMPLE C (Test 1, Question 6: Email to Max)

> Hi Max,
> I enjoy very much to invite you to go with me to the golf club next Saturday I have just found a golf club in my area and I'll be pleasure if you accept to visit the club with me. If you accept the invitation call me please.
> Thanks
> Vera

Examiner Comments

The first two elements are adequately dealt with, but the third (say what you could do there together) is only implied by the content of the first two elements. The message also requires some effort by the reader.

Band: 3

Part 3

The following sample answers and commentaries should be read in conjunction with the General Mark scheme for **Writing Part 3** given on page 14–15.

SAMPLE D (Test 1, Question 7: Letter to a friend)

Hi Bob,

There are so many traditional festivals in my country. They depend on the area and they are different according to the season, people etc......

The most important one of them is Da Gubal – festival. People celebrate this festival every 10th May to honor Mong-Ju princess who lived in Sila Kingdom that was name of Korea long time ago.

One day she fell in love with someone who was prince of opponent country. He loved her as well but they didn't get married. At the same time their country was in the war. He asked her to deliver information about her army.

She was worring about it. Finally she decided that she would betray him. Therefore her country won in the war

See you soon

Kim

Examiner Comments

This is a very good attempt at the task, showing confident and natural use of language. The letter is informative and requires no effort by the reader. There is a wide range of structures and vocabulary, occasionally above PET level, for example *according to the season... she would betray him.* Errors are minor, due to ambition and non-impeding, for example *that was name of Korea long time ago.*

Band: 5

SAMPLE E (Test 1, Question 7: Letter to a friend)

Dear Jonh,

I have received your letter and am very happy to get yours news. So, I want to tell you something more importante. It' is a traditional festivals in my city. Will be start on next week. It is a kind of traditional music. People are making an exibition dance with many musical instruments. I will have a good time, so I thing, I am going to take some photos for you and you can see, which impression you can do. This moment will be fantastic for verybody.

I suggest you if you can come with us in this special occasion. You don't feel awful or worring about. It is a sensational african music, women are dancing a lovely song and wear sexy clothes. It is beautiful to see this spectacle in live, no, to hear. Think you very much for your letter, it is my pleasure to read you soon. Bye

Yours friend.

Examiner Comments

This is an ambitious attempt at the task, showing some range of vocabulary. The letter has a friendly tone and gives a lot of information to the friend. However, it is flawed by a high number of mainly non-impeding errors, particularly in spelling, agreement, and use of prepositions, for example *it is a traditional festivals... this spectacle in live, no, to hear*.

Band: 3

SAMPLE F (Test 1, Question 7: Letter to a friend)

Hello Matin,

How are you? I'm fine. I want to meet you. I think we have a new years. It is the most important day. Because of they want to talking about this year's plan and didn't tell anything for a while. We would buy new cloth and meet relative and would go to grand father's tomb. If you have a festival, could you tell me something?

Friendly Denny

Examiner Comments

This is a poor attempt, which is difficult to understand at times, because of impeding errors, for example *I think we have a new years. …they want to talking about this year's plan and didn't tell anything for a while.* It is also too short at 69 words long and so receives a mark in Band 1.

Band: 1

SAMPLE G (Test 1, Question 8: Nobody knew what Adam had in his suitcase.)

Nobody knew what adam had in his suitcase. One day, sunshine day in Brugges away to Germany adam house, he decided go to Brugges because he wrotte a poem about this place, he got the suitcase and put in, one picture he's camara, silvee neckles, a tape, two T-short, one jeans because hi's a jornalist of National Geografic, Hi like wild life, in there he met with a beautiful girl her name is Esmeralda and he asked her for the Maddison Bridge, she said is very difficult explain, I have to go with you he said ok when he got this place hi said the must beautiful I can see in my life. He said I wish take a picture with you on the Bridge, she said not I am not pretty he said I like natural impresion. She got red all face, and he said you are lady in my picture which brought in my suitcase do you want to see, look is you oh my got a can't beleve and Adam and Esmeralda lieve together for ever.

Examiner Comments

Although an ambitious attempt at story-telling, this answer is held in Band 2 because of its numerous errors, especially in sentence structure, past tenses, spelling and punctuation. Some errors impede understanding, for example *…he's camara, silvee neckles, a tape, two T-short, one jeans because hi's a …*

Band: 2

SAMPLE H (Test 1, Question 8: Nobody knew what Adam had in his suitcase.)

Nobody knew what Adam had in his suitcase. It was black big suitcase with silver belts he took it ever day and never left it. But the worst day for Adam have came. He lost his suitcase at the Stansted Airport. He put it only for a second and when he back the suitcase disapeared. He has looked for it everywhere but nobody saw this suitcase. Adam made a decision I had to go to police station and saw them about this case. He was very sad because it was his best suitcase like best friend and he miss a them. He was sitting at the Airport and he remembered that he had a his name address and number of his mobile phone on his suitcase. Suddenly he heard that his phone was ringing and he took it up and heard one woman had his lugage and he could took it from Hilton Hotel in London room. It was beatiful women. She sed that she didn't know how this happened but she took it Adam. Thanks you and invite her to very nice reataurant. They fall in love immidetly and got married next month. I'm this son and i tell you this story because it's very funny.
Take care
Dominik

Examiner Comments

This is another ambitious attempt at a story, which is longer than 100 words but not penalised for this, as the text is relevant. Some range is shown, for example *Adam made a decision… Suddenly he heard that his phone was ringing…* but there are also a high number of non-impeding errors, for example *But the worst day for Adam have came. They fall in love immidetly…*

Band: 3

SAMPLE I (Test 1, Question 8: Nobody knew what Adam had in his suitcase.)

> Nobody knew what Adam had in his suitase.
> Adam always went to somewhere with his suitcase but nobody saw when he opened it. For example he took his suitcase to work. He was a secretary and he just answered the calls. The suitcase always stood under the table at his work.
> He took the suitcase to the disco and danced near it. He always looked after the suitcase.
> And when somebody asked him what was in the suitcase he said that there was nothing interesting in the suitcase.

Examiner Comments

This is a fairly unambitious attempt, but it is virtually error-free and shows some evidence of structural range, for example *...when somebody asked him what was in the suitcase...* . The script just reaches the minimum acceptable length of 80 words (excluding the given sentence).

Band: 4

PAPER 2   LISTENING

Part 1

1 B   2 A   3 C   4 B   5 C   6 C   7 A

Part 2

8 B   9 B   10 C   11 A   12 C   13 B

Part 3

14   Monday afternoon/p.m.
15   America / U.S.A. / United States (of America)
16   £1.75
17   tourist office(s)
18   beach
19   computer(s)

Part 4

20 B   21 A   22 A   23 B   24 A   25 A

Test 1 transcript

This is the Cambridge Preliminary English Test number 1. There are four parts to the test. You will hear each part twice.

For each part of the test, there will be time for you to look through the questions and time for you to check your answers.

Write your answers on the question paper. You will have six minutes at the end of the test to copy your answers onto the answer sheet.

The recording will now be stopped. Please ask any questions now, because you must not speak during the test.

[pause]

Now open your question paper and look at Part 1.

PART 1   *There are seven questions in this part. For each question there are three pictures and a short recording. Choose the correct picture and put a tick in the box below it.*

Before we start, here is an example.

Where did the man leave his camera?

Man: Oh no! I haven't got my camera!
Woman: But you used it just now to take a photograph of the fountain.
Man: Oh I remember, I put it down on the steps while I put my coat on.
Woman: Well, let's drive back quickly – it might still be there.

[pause]

The first picture is correct so there is a tick in box A.

Look at the three pictures for Question 1 now.

[pause]

Now we are ready to start. Listen carefully. You will hear each recording twice.

One. Which activity will the family do this year?

Woman: We're going to try an activity holiday this year, but we all want to do something different. The children want to go cycling but their father wants to go on a water sports holiday, you know, sailing and windsurfing, things like that. And I'd like to go walking. We all want to go together so we've decided to let the children choose this year, and we'll choose next year.

[pause]

Now listen again.

[The recording is repeated.]

[pause]

Two. Which is the woman's house?

Man: How will I recognise your house when I call for you, Sue?
Woman: Well, it's the same as all the others in the street, but look out for a big tree. It's by the front gate and it's covered in lovely white flowers at the moment.

[pause]

Now listen again.

[The recording is repeated.]

[pause]

Three. Why will drivers have problems this morning?

Man: And on to this morning's local traffic news. Driving conditions have improved now that the early morning fog has gone. Rain is forecast for tonight but it will be fine during the day. The police have warned drivers to expect delays coming into town because of repairs to Victoria Bridge and advise lorries to find another route if possible.

[pause]

Now listen again.

[The recording is repeated.]

[pause]

Four. What time will Robin leave the house?

Woman: Oh Robin! Pete's just rung to say that he'll be here a bit later than he said. The plane's going to take off at eight o'clock now so you don't need to check-in until about quarter past seven. He said he'd be round to pick you up at half past six instead of six o'clock. Is that OK? It'll give you some more time to pack anyway!

[pause]

Now listen again.

[The recording is repeated.]

[pause]

Five. What did Simon do this morning?

Woman: Oh Simon, you haven't even washed the dishes. Have you done anything this morning?

Boy: I've been really busy, Mum. I paid the window cleaner who called and I was going to put away all the shopping you bought yesterday but Pete rang and he kept me talking for ages.

[pause]

Now listen again.

[The recording is repeated.]

[pause]

Six. What hasn't the girl packed yet?

Woman: Have you got everything you need for your holiday?

Girl: Well, I've packed my soap and toothbrush if that's what you mean, but I can't find any toothpaste anywhere.

Woman: There's probably some in the bathroom cupboard. But what about a towel, have you remembered to pack that?

Girl: Of course.

[pause]

Now listen again.

[The recording is repeated.]

[pause]

Seven. What has the woman just bought?

Woman: What do you think? I found it in that new department store yesterday. I think it's perfect. It'll keep the sun off my face and it'll go really well with the dress I'm wearing to the wedding. It's the same colour as my bag, too. I just need a new jacket now.

[pause]

Now listen again.

[The recording is repeated.]

[pause]

That is the end of Part 1.

[pause]

PART 2   *Now turn to Part 2, questions 8–13.*

You will hear an interview with Angela Morgan, who has recently flown around the world in a helicopter.
For each question, put a tick in the correct box. You now have 45 seconds to look at the questions for Part 2.

[pause]

Now we are ready to start. Listen carefully. You will hear the recording twice.

Man: And today I'm talking to Angela Morgan. Angela, what made you decide to fly round the world in a helicopter?

Woman: People often ask me <u>why</u> I decided to do it but I'm surprised they don't ask 'Why did you wait so long?' because I'm 57 now! I'm sorry I didn't do it <u>years</u> ago, because it was such a wonderful experience. But the main purpose for going was to collect £500,000 for sick children by getting different companies to pay us money for each kilometre that we flew.

Man: And now everyone calls you the flying grandmother!

Woman: Yes, the thing about growing older is that you don't feel any different inside, so you have to do as much as you can while you can. I'm healthy, and my own children are grown up, so I was free to go.

Man: And what about preparing for the trip?

Woman: Well, it took five months to plan. I <u>was</u> going to go with my husband, but he couldn't take time off work. Instead I made the trip with my flying teacher who became a great friend while she was teaching me to fly three years ago. I passed my flying test after two weeks; found it quite easy.

Man: And what was the trip like?

Woman: It was really exciting flying over so many different countries. The only thing was that we weren't able to spend much time sightseeing because we only stopped to get water and to camp. We took very little with us, but we did have tents and cooking things to use at night. We had to spend two days in Thailand because of an engine problem, but that was the longest we spent anywhere. Fortunately nothing else went wrong, so we just kept on going after that.

Man: What did you enjoy most about the trip?

Woman: The most wonderful thing about flying was seeing the differences in the countryside as we flew across 26 countries in 97 days. We flew over oceans and close to mountains; sometimes it was quite frightening, but we didn't travel when it was dark. We spent several nights camping in the desert and the sky was just full of stars. I made a video of the trip; you'll see it in a minute.

Man: Was there anything that you missed while you were away?

Woman: Well, to my surprise I didn't miss going to work or going out to restaurants or films. The most difficult thing was sitting still all the time; I normally play tennis and swim several times a week, so I started to feel very unfit. I missed hot water and proper showers sometimes too, but not as much as I thought I would!

[pause]

Now listen again.

[The recording is repeated.]

That is the end of Part 2.

[pause]

PART 3   *Now turn to Part 3, questions 14–19.*

You will hear a radio announcer talking about activities at a museum called Science World.

For each question, fill in the missing information in the numbered space. You now have 20 seconds to look at Part 3.

[pause]

Now we are ready to start. Listen carefully. You will hear the recording twice.

Man: This week in the local activities part of the show, we're taking a look at Science World, the new place to visit for a family day out. During your visit you'll be able to find out about all the latest developments in science, as well as trying lots of experiments for yourself. This is no ordinary museum, I promise you! There's a programme of special events, which next week includes an Electricity Workshop on Monday afternoon, and the chance to do some experiments with water on Wednesday morning. Of special interest is the regular Saturday evening talk: next week Science World welcomes a famous American scientist who is going to talk about space travel.

It isn't expensive to visit Science World, with tickets priced at three pounds for adults and two pounds for children. Talks and other special events are extra, though, with an entrance fee of £1.75 for adults and there are reductions for children. If you want to go to a special event or talk, then book your tickets direct from Science World on 284311, or pick them up from the tourist office.

While you're at Science World, you'll be able to enjoy a snack in the Newton Café – it's a bit small, but the food is good. It's open all day and it has a lovely view because it's beside the beach.

Still not sure? Well, why not give Science World a call on 284311? If you say you heard about Science World on this programme they will send you one free ticket to next month's exhibition which is about computers. It's suitable for families and school parties.

And now let's look at …

[pause]

Now listen again.

[The recording is repeated.]

That is the end of Part 3.

[pause]

PART 4   *Now turn to Part 4, questions 20–25.*

Look at the six sentences for this part. You will hear a conversation between a boy, Tom, and his sister, Clare, about school.
Decide if each sentence is correct or incorrect. If it is correct, put a tick in the box under A for YES. If it is not correct, put a tick in the box under B for NO. You now have 20 seconds to look at the questions for Part 4.

[pause]

Now we are ready to start. Listen carefully. You will hear the recording twice.

Boy: Guess what, Clare? I've been chosen for the school swimming team! What do you think about that?

Girl: Well, I think it's great, but I'm sure Dad won't say the same when he finds out. You know how he feels about you doing all this sport and not doing your school work. You'll never get all your homework done, especially if you have to travel to other schools for competitions.

Boy: It won't make any difference. I can do my homework on the bus.

Girl: Honestly Tom, you know what your teacher said to Dad last term. You've got a good brain and you could improve your marks at school if you spent a bit less time thinking about sport. Sometimes I wonder if you ever think about anything else at all.

Boy: Well, I work hard at everything I like doing, not just sport. I mean, take maths for example.

Girl: Okay, it's your life, but you know you have your examinations next year for college, and at most of the good colleges they have great sports facilities. If you aren't accepted, then you'll have to find a job and that won't be easy.

Boy: Oh I've thought about that already. I'm thinking of applying to do Sports Science at college and someone told me some of the colleges often take students with lower marks if they're good at sport.

Girl: Well, I wouldn't depend on what one of your friends says if I were you.

Boy: For your information it wasn't one of my friends, it was a teacher at school.

Girl: I'm only trying to help and anyway it doesn't really matter what I say, it's Dad you have to worry about.

Boy: Yes, okay. I know you're right about <u>that</u>. I'll have a chat with him tonight and explain things again.

Girl: Good luck!

[pause]

Now listen again.

[The recording is repeated.]

That is the end of Part 4.

[pause]

You now have six minutes to check and copy your answers onto the answer sheet.

Note: Teacher, stop the recording here and time six minutes. Remind students when there is **one** minute remaining.

That is the end of the test.

Test 2

PAPER 1   READING AND WRITING

READING

Part 1

1 B   2 A   3 B   4 C   5 C

Part 2

6 D   7 B   8 A   9 E   10 F

Part 3

| 11 A | 12 A | 13 B | 14 A | 15 B | 16 A | 17 B |
| 18 A | 19 B | 20 A |

Part 4

21 D   22 D   23 C   24 B   25 C

Part 5

| 26 B | 27 C | 28 D | 29 A | 30 B | 31 C | 32 B |
| 33 D | 34 B | 35 A |

WRITING

Part 1

1 Maria lives a long way from her office.

| **Maria's office isn't** | (situated/located) close to / near (to) | **her home.** |

2 It is a forty-minute bus journey to her office.

| **The bus journey to her office** | takes (her) / lasts/is (about) | **forty minutes.** |

3 Driving a car in the town centre is not allowed.

| **You are not allowed** | to drive | **cars in the town centre.** |

4 Maria sometimes takes a taxi although it is expensive.

| **Maria doesn't often take a taxi** | as/since/because | **it is expensive.** |

5 Yesterday she got up too late to catch the bus.

Yesterday she got up so late that she	missed OR didn't / couldn't / failed to catch/take/get	the bus.

Part 2

The Task-specific Mark scheme given below should be used in conjunction with the General Mark scheme for **Writing Part 2** given on page 13.

Task-specific Mark scheme

The content elements that need to be covered are:

i   an invitation to your friend to the party
ii information on when it will take place
iii a reason why you want to surprise your cousin

The following sample answers can be used as a guide when marking.

SAMPLE A (Test 2, Question 6: Card to a friend)

> Would you mind welcome to my party? This is a surprise party for my cousin. I'd like to surprise her that I'll make the big cake, and put it into the ring for present. I'll take my house and stat at 7:00 pm

Examiner Comments

All three content elements are unsuccessfully dealt with: there is no clear invitation, no explanation of why the writer wants to surprise the cousin and the information about when the party will take place only includes a time. The message also requires excessive effort to understand, for example *Would you mind welcome to my party? I'll take my house and stat at…*

Band: 1

SAMPLE B (Test 2, Question 6: Card to a friend)

Mr. Paul Dunn

Dear Paul:

I am really glad to invite you to my cousin "birthday's party". He is 6 years old and admires you a lot, because always you have been so friendly with him. The meeting will be in my house at 3:00pm. Our address is:

46 Nibthwaite Road

Harrow — Middlesex

You could take the Metro-politan line to "Harrow on the Hill" and I enclose a map if you request.

Don't forget come with your daughter Julie. Michie will have a surprise when he will see again to Julie!!!

Yours, Sincerelly

Maria Cuisans

Examiner Comments

Although the candidate has attempted the content points, the explanation why is unclear and there is inadequate information about when the party will take place. The answer is also too long due to the extra information about how to get to the house, which is irrelevant to the task set.

Band: 2

SAMPLE C (Test 2, Question 6: Card to a friend)

Dear Jim

How have you been recently? Did you remember my cousin James? Now he is ten years old. Next Sunday we will having a birthday party for him. As you know, he thinks you are the greatest magican in the whole world. So hope you can come here next Sunday. Show your fantistic magic, give him a surprise.

If you could, James must feel so happy.

Love

Tommy

Examiner Comments

This is a very good attempt, covering all content elements appropriately. Although the candidate has exceeded the word limit, the expansion is relevant to the invitation. Minor language errors are present, but do not impair the clarity of the message.

Band: 5

Part 3

The following sample answers and commentaries should be read in conjunction with the General Mark scheme for **Writing Part 3** given on pages 14–15.

SAMPLE D (Test 2, Question 7: Letter to a friend)

> Hi I used a computer for a couple of years rather to work than play. It's helped me with my firm to account. So when I spent a lot of time face to face with a monitor I felt really upset to spent more just for a game. I'd rather prefer in my off days cycling and all activity sports My eyes need to see something more not just slashing pictures. But of course some-times when the weather is really boring (raining, winding etc) I'd like to lay at home and play to strategic game. My best is Civilisation it isn't just blood and meat everywhere. Good luck with your new amusments.
> Bye, Anders

Examiner Comments

This is a good attempt, showing fairly good control and ambitious use of language. The letter is well organised on the whole and there is some evidence of range of structures and vocabulary. Errors are non-impeding, for example *I'd rather prefer in my off days... raining, winding, etc.*

Band: 4

SAMPLE E (Test 2, Question 7: Letter to a friend)

I am very glad, that you have bought a new computer game. What's a pity, that I can not talk witch you about it!
I don't know anything about computers, games and I don't know exactelly what is this — Play Station:). Sometimes I go to internet café in order to send e-mail to my friends and sister in Poland. I can use internet explorer and I am afraid this is all I can do with computers. And I don't like any computer games (maybe because of this I have not too much occasions to check it:).
I prefer to write an ordinary letters like this one. In this matter I am a tradicionalist. Yours faithfully....

Examiner Comments

This is an adequate attempt at the task showing some control of language, although linking is not always maintained. There is no opening formula and a number of non-impeding errors occur, mainly in spelling and use of articles, for example *exactelly… an ordinary letters… too much occasions.*

Band: 3

SAMPLE F (Test 2, Question 7: Letter to a friend)

Dear Petter

I have got your letter to day at 11.30 am. How are you? Is doing fine. I am quit busy right now. I have much to do for my schoole. Soon I'll have an exame. I have to work hard in the moment. Most of time after schoole I stay in laibrery. I haven't been out since last month.

You told me that you have got a new computer game. What's it supriseing. I think that is wonderfull.

My computer is too old. It was for my brother. I am not using it often, just some times I use it for my school work. It hasn't got exciting games.

I hopp I'll get new computer soon which is letest and can use for evrything. This is my short letter, but I'll write you more next time.

Yours truly,

Yordanos

Examiner Comments

This is an inadequate attempt, which introduces substantial digression in the first half of the script before dealing with the task. It is better for candidates to focus on the topic required, rather than insert 'pre-learned' paragraphs like this. There are numerous errors, though these are mainly in spelling and are non-impeding, for example *What's it surpriseing. …which is latest and can use for evrything.*

Band: 2

SAMPLE G (Test 2, Question 8: Winning the prize)

Dear Kate:

I 'am really sorry because I can't come to class this week, but I had a new for you: I tell you what happened: "I winning the prize"!!! You know, I was practising swimming a lot, this time and I had a competition in Cambrigde! The week was hardest because all our teem work lots. We were practice 4 hours per day and after out training we went to visit a lot of museums, theater, parks, etc.

I enjoy that time.

I hope you understand my absences but I retorn to your class again

Thank you so much

Maria

Examiner Comments

This is an inadequate attempt, showing some misunderstanding of the task set (the candidate has written a letter to her teacher about winning a prize). The language is fairly limited and contains numerous errors, particularly in past tenses, for example …*all our teem work lots. We were practice… I retorn to your class again.*

Band: 2

SAMPLE H (Test 2, Question 8: Winning the prize)

I don't know how it happened! I have never been lucky in any lotteries, games etc. And suddenly I recived o notice from the American Ambassy that I have won a Green Card! This is impossible! One year ago I sent an application to Green Card lottery, but I didn't think about it later. I had sent it, because my friend which were with me in America told me about this, and I have known people, who had a Green card from lottery.

This is a very nice suprise for me, because USA is my favorite place since I was there two years ago. I would never think that I could come back there.

Examiner Comments

This is a very good attempt, showing confident and ambitious use of language, with a wide range of structures and vocabulary. Errors are minor and due to this ambition, for example *…my friend which were with me in America told me about this.*

Band: 5

SAMPLE I (Test 2, Question 8: Winning the prize)

> Winning the prize. My last holiday I spent with my friends in Spain. The holiday was very, very nice. We were in Spain two weeks. Very often we went to the restaurent. Last day we went to Chine restaurent. Before I never heve been in Chine resteurent. This evening wes very excating for us. In this restaurent was the careoce. In this day someone can win the prize. The prize was a big toy. My friend Tommy is not a good singer, but he is funny. His the song wesn't well. Everybody couldn't heer him. The own of the restaurent gave him the prize, becous he wes funny. Last day in Spain I'll remember.

Examiner Comments

This is an adequate attempt, with evidence of some control of language. Simple sentence structure is sound, but there are a number of mostly non-impeding errors, especially in spelling, word order and use of articles, for example *Before I never heve been in Chine resteurent. His the song wesn't well.*

Band: 3

Key

Part 1

1 B   2 B   3 A   4 A   5 B   6 C   7 C

Part 2

8 A   9 C   10 C   11 A   12 A   13 C

Part 3

14   expensive / not cheap

15   Square / Sq

16   (the) (bus) driver(s)

17   map(s)

18   jewellery

19   a quarter to five / four forty(-)five / 16.45 / 4:45

Part 4

20 B   21 B   22 B   23 A   24 A   25 B

Test 2 transcript

This is the Cambridge Preliminary English Test number 2. There are four parts to the test. You will hear each part twice.

For each part of the test, there will be time for you to look through the questions and time for you to check your answers.

Write your answers on the question paper. You will have six minutes at the end of the test to copy your answers onto the answer sheet.

The recording will now be stopped. Please ask any questions now, because you must not speak during the test.

[pause]

Now open your question paper and look at Part 1.

[pause]

PART 1   *There are seven questions in this part. For each question there are three pictures and a short recording. Choose the correct picture and put a tick in the box below it.*

Before we start, here is an example.

What's the time?

Woman Have you got the time?

Man: Yes, it's twenty past three.

[pause]

The first picture is correct so there is a tick in box A.

Look at the three pictures for Question 1 now.

[pause]

Now we are ready to start. Listen carefully. You will hear each recording twice.

One. How much is the man's ticket?

Man: Can you tell me how much a ticket is for Saturday's performance of Macbeth?

Woman: The front stalls and the circle are the most expensive at £16.50. The middle seats in the stalls cost £15 and the back three rows cost £12.50, but the view isn't so good. All seats are £10 for students.

Man: I'll have one in the middle please. I'm not a student. I've got my credit card here …

[pause]

Now listen again.

[The recording is repeated.]

[pause]

Two. What will they have for lunch?

Man: It's chips for lunch. What would you like with them?

Woman: Not fish again, please, and we had chicken last night.

Man: Well, we've got plenty of sausages, but we've finished the eggs, I'm afraid.

Woman: That's decided then.

[pause]

Now listen again.

[The recording is repeated.]

[pause]

Three. Why was the man late home?

Woman: Hi! Have you had a busy day at the office?

Man: Yes, sorry I'm late. I didn't get the bus because Pete offered me a lift. We didn't realise the motorway was closed because of a lorry accident, so it took much longer than normal. I'll be even later tomorrow with the train strike.

[pause]

Now listen again.

[The recording is repeated.]

[pause]

Four. What was the weather like on John's holiday?

Man 1: How was your holiday, John?

Man 2: We had a good time, but the weather was awful. We didn't have one sunny day!

Man 1: Oh dear, a week in the rain, poor you.

Man 2: Well, that's the funny thing. It never actually rained, it was just freezing cold and cloudy, we thought it might even snow.

[pause]

Now listen again.

[The recording is repeated.]

[pause]

Five. What time was the woman's appointment?

Woman: I've had an awful morning! I was really late for my hospital appointment. I just missed the 9 o'clock bus, and the next one didn't come until 20 to 10. I was supposed to see the doctor at 10 past 10, but I didn't arrive until half past. He wasn't very pleased.

[pause]

Now listen again.

[The recording is repeated.]

[pause]

Six. What did the woman buy?

Man: Did you get anything from the duty-free shop?

Woman: Well, I really wanted some of that perfume I bought last time and I got a large bottle. Then I looked for the walkman I'd promised I'd get for Tony. Fortunately, they'd sold all of them, so I had enough money for a lovely silk scarf for myself. I completely forgot about the chocolates I was supposed to get for Mary.

[pause]

Now listen again.

[The recording is repeated.]

[pause]

Seven. Where are the man and the woman talking?

Woman: It's a bit crowded isn't it … worse than a football match! Can you see well enough from here?

Man: It doesn't matter – as long as I can hear and get down the important points of what he says, it's OK.

Woman: I'm going to the library after this. I want to get this report finished so that I can go to the cinema.

[pause]

Now listen again.

[The recording is repeated.]

[pause]

That is the end of Part 1.

[pause]

PART 2 *Now turn to Part 2, questions 8–13.*

You will hear a woman called Sarah talking to a group of people about her painting.
For each question, put a tick in the correct box. You now have 45 seconds to look at the questions for Part 2.

[pause]

Now we are ready to start. Listen carefully. You will hear the recording twice.

Woman: Well, good evening everyone. I've come along to talk to you about my painting. It <u>was</u> just a hobby but it's really more than that now. I used to paint in the evenings after work, but now I work four days a week instead of five. That means I spend Friday, Saturday and Sunday on my painting. I have pictures in local exhibitions at least once a month.

I'd love to give up my job and spend all my time painting, but I work with computers and I earn more that way! I do make <u>some</u> money from selling my pictures, enough to pay for all my paint, brushes and paper and a few art lessons. I'd love to go to art college full-time for three years, but I've got all the rent on my flat to pay and a car to run.

I first became interested in art when I was at primary school. I used to go out with some paper and a few pencils during break time and draw anything I saw: houses, gardens, people. Then at secondary school we had art classes twice a week, and I learnt how to use chalk and then different kinds of paint: water colours, oils and so on.

Those classes were really useful for me, and ever since then I've had lessons of some kind. I've attended evening classes and been on what they call painting 'holidays', where you go out into the countryside and paint during the day and then sit and discuss your work with a teacher and the other artists after dinner. Those holidays are great; you learn so much talking to other people studying with you.

I've enjoyed painting in lots of different countries. I've been to Morocco and painted desert scenes with beautiful sunrises. I've been to Greece and Spain and painted pictures of the local people working in the fields near their homes. My favourite place is still Scotland. I love walking in the Scottish mountains, and there are so many different birds to see, especially in spring.

Well, I'm going to finish now by showing you a video of the places I've visited. After that there'll be a chance to relax with a cup of coffee and then there'll be time for some questions. Oh, and I've got some information about my next art exhibition for you. It's going to be at the Queen's Gallery. Now, if someone would turn off the lights …

[pause]

Now listen again.

[The recording is repeated.]

That is the end of Part 2.

[pause]

PART 3   *Now turn to Part 3, questions 14–19.*

You will hear a radio programme giving you information about the city of Glasgow.
For each question, fill in the missing information in the numbered space. You now have 20 seconds to look at Part 3.

[pause]

Now we are ready to start. Listen carefully. You will hear the recording twice.

Man: Well, good morning. This week's programme is about the city of Glasgow. We're going to give you some ideas of what you can see and do if you visit for a weekend. Glasgow is Britain's third largest city, and Scotland's biggest. It is well worth a visit.

If you arrive by car, the motorway will take you into the city centre. Don't park in one of the city centre car parks however, as they are expensive. It's better to leave your car at your hotel or somewhere away from the centre, and take the bus.

Glasgow is a large city and there is an excellent public transport system. A good idea is to catch a "Discovering Glasgow" tour bus which leaves George Square every half hour. You can get off anywhere and catch the next bus to continue your trip. The tour costs £5 and tickets are available from the bus driver.

If you want to walk around the city centre, then it's best to start at the Welcome Centre on St Vincent Place. You can get information about opening times and entrance fees of places to visit and take a free map to help you with your sightseeing.

Don't miss the fifteenth century cathedral, which has particularly beautiful windows. Further on is the Merchant City area, where there are cafés and lots of small, fashionable shops which sell jewellery and clothes.

Byres Road is popular with university students and you can find a lot of bargains in the shops around there. The Botanic Gardens are also worth a visit. The gardens are open until sunset, and the glasshouses from ten o'clock until a quarter to five. These contain a wide variety of beautiful plants and flowers. The gardens are also a good place to have a picnic.

Well …

[pause]

Now listen again.

[The recording is repeated.]

That is the end of Part 3.

[pause]

PART 4   *Now turn to Part 4, questions 20–25.*

Look at the six sentences for this part. You will hear a conversation between a boy, Frank, and a girl, Linda, in a music shop.
Decide if each sentence is correct or incorrect. If it is correct, put a tick in the box under A for YES. If it is not correct, put a tick in the box under B for NO. You now have 20 seconds to look at the questions for Part 4.

[pause]

Now we are ready to start. Listen carefully. You will hear the recording twice.

Boy: So, where do you want to go first, Linda?
Girl: Let's go in here. I want to see what they've got. It was my birthday last week and Mum gave me some cassettes. They're really great but I've already got one of them so I want to change it for something else.
Boy: I love this shop, there's always so much to choose from. What are you going to get?
Girl: I'm not sure. I thought I'd just have a look around and see if there's anything I like the look of. I want something different. I'm a bit bored with all the music I normally listen to. Can you suggest anything?
Boy: Well, you don't usually like the sort of music I listen to. What about this band?
Girl: Who are they? I've never heard of them.
Boy: They're a new band from America. They're not very well known yet but you wait and see. In another couple of years they'll be really famous.
Girl: Mmm, let me have a look. Can you find it on cassette for me? I haven't got a CD player.
Boy: The sound's much better on a CD, you should get one.
Girl: Well, there's no point for me, my cassette player's really good quality, so it wouldn't make any difference. Besides CDs cost a lot more than cassettes.
Boy: Here you are. I've found it on cassette.
Girl: Oh look, it's on special offer. That's really cheap, isn't it? I'll take it.
Boy: There's something else we could get while we're here.

Girl: What's that?

Boy: Well, there's a concert in the sports stadium next week. There's a new Irish band playing. You might like them, so would you like to come with me?

Girl: That sounds great. I hope I do like them. The last band you took me to see was awful.

Boy: This one is different. I'll go and buy some tickets then, shall I?

Girl: All right then.

[pause]

Now listen again.

[The recording is repeated.]

That is the end of Part 4.

[pause]

You now have six minutes to check and copy your answers onto the answer sheet.

Note: Teacher, stop the recording here and time six minutes. Remind students when there is **one** minute remaining.

That is the end of the test.

Test 3

PAPER 1   READING AND WRITING

READING

Part 1

1 C   2 B   3 B   4 A   5 C

Part 2

6 E   7 A   8 C   9 F   10 G

Part 3

| 11 A | 12 B | 13 A | 14 A | 15 A | 16 A | 17 A |
| 18 B | 19 B | 20 B | | | | |

Part 4

21 A   22 C   23 D   24 B   25 C

Part 5

| 26 C | 27 D | 28 B | 29 A | 30 A | 31 D | 32 C |
| 33 B | 34 C | 35 C | | | | |

WRITING

Part 1

1 Large cars use more petrol than small cars.

| **Small cars don't use as** | much petrol as | **large cars.** |

2 Check your tyres before a long journey.

| **Before a long journey, remember** | to check | **your tyres.** |

3 When I was young, I drove a small car.

| **I used to** | drive | **a small car when I was young.** |

4 My car windscreen was broken by a stone.

| **A stone** | broke | **my car windscreen.** |

5 Who does this van belong to?

Whose	van is	**this?**

Part 2

The Task-specific Mark scheme given below should be used in conjunction with the General Mark scheme for **Writing Part 2** given on page 13.

Task-specific Mark scheme

The content elements that need to be covered are:

i   a request for Pat to join you at the concert this evening
ii information on where the concert will take place
iii information about what sort of music will be performed

The following sample answers can be used as a guide when marking.

SAMPLE A (Test 3, Question 6: Note to Pat)

Hi Pat,
I am going to invite you go to a concert with me this evening. The concert place just near your house. Can you wait for me in the xxx street? Pop music will be performed. I'm hoping you enjoy it.
Your friend
Jiang
Nov 20th

Examiner Comments

All three content elements are adequately dealt with and the message is communicated successfully on the whole, but language errors require a little effort by the reader.

Band: 4

SAMPLE B (Test 3, Question 6: Note to Pat)

> Do you have a plenty of time this evening? Because I am going to go to a concert this evening with a group of friends and I want to you come too.
>
> When you will go there with me maybe you will have a nice time. You take a 6 of bus and then come to the Picadilly tube station. We are waiting for you until 7.00pm. I don't know but someone said to me they have got perfect harmoney.

Examiner Comments

This is an inadequate attempt, as the candidate has responded to the bullet points instead of writing a cohesive note to a friend, which leads to only partial realisation of the task (the second and third elements are unsuccessfully addressed).

Band: 2

SAMPLE C (Test 3, Question 6: Note to Pat)

> Hello Pat! I and some friends are going to a concert tonight. I let you this message to ask you to join us. The concert will take place at Stratford's shopping centre at 9pm. It will be a Jazz concert
>
> See you tonight!

Examiner Comments

All content elements are covered appropriately in a clearly communicated message. Language errors are minor and require no effort by the reader.

Band: 5

Part 3

The following sample answers and commentaries should be read in conjunction with the General Mark scheme for **Writing Part 3** given on pages 14–15.

SAMPLE D (Test 3, Question 7: I was standing beside someone famous!)

> I was standing beside someone famous! I was so excited that during a few seconds I couldn't do anything. I was standing and loocked him. He was more taller and more beautiful that he seemed on TV.
>
> Suddenly he turned his head and fixed me. I was petrified! He smiled and said hello. I opened my mouth but I couldn't say something. He asked me how I found the show. Finaly I answered him. I said it was great. I added that I loved his music and particular his last album. I asked him to sign me an autograph the he shaked my hand and went.

Examiner Comments

This is a very good attempt, showing confident use of language and a wide range of vocabulary, for example *Suddenly he turned his head... I was petrified*. Errors are minor and mostly due to ambition, for example *I added that I loved his music and particular his last album*. The story is also well organised and requires no effort to read.

Band: 5

SAMPLE E (Test 3, Question 7: I was standing beside someone famous!)

I was standing beside someone famous! I could't belive! I was doing the shopping, like every Saturday, you know boring life.....But in one time I see Madonna is trying new dress! First time I thout. No it's impossible! Madonna doing shoping in the same Supermarket like me?! But it was trou! She came for the premiere new Band! It was emaising! First time in my life I'm met someon famous! (exclusive TV). This boring day was changing and stay one of the most exciting in my life! No I know every next day can give me someting new, very interesting experience. I'm very happy I arrived to London! This is fantastic city!

Examiner Comments

This is an ambitious and lively attempt at telling a story, which is flawed by a number of mostly non-impeding errors, for example *I could't belive… Madonna is trying new dress. It was emaising!* Two errors impede understanding: *(exclusive TV)… No I know every next day…*

Band: 3

SAMPLE F (Test 3, Question 7: I was standing beside someone famous!)

I was standing beside someone famous!
It was long tome ago I saw o the strreet Elton Jon I
was suprice, and shocked because he set hello to me
and how are you, he was really friendli, I don't now way
I felt sow heppe because I met someon famous.
London is a very big city, is posible to see e lot of
famous pepul.

Examiner Comments

This is an inadequate attempt, which is only 60 words long. The language is fairly limited and repetitive, and errors often occur in the spelling of PET-level words, for example *he set hello... I felt sow heppe... famous pepul.*

Band: 2

SAMPLE G (Test 3, Question 8: Letter to a friend)

Hi! How are you? Are you all right? I'm fine. Is it very hot in Australia now? Now my country is coming the winter. It is cold everyday. I went to Mt. Fuji last week. It was very very cold. But I enjoyed to climb up Mt. Fuji! After 2 months, I will go to snow mountains because I can play "Snow board". When I was 17 years old I begun to play it. I can play it very well I think. I have never been in Australia but I watched on TV about Australia. I think Australia is hot whole year! Is this truth? Please tell me and I have never played surfing please teach me. I'd like to play surfing! If you could to Japan, I can take you all Japan. Now Japan is fall! I want t take to the mountains because it is very beautiful the mountains. The leaf is changing from green to red or yellow! Can you imagine like New England area? The same! Anyway I enjoy to go all of Japan. Have a good time. I hope you will be happy! Take care! Bye!

Examiner Comments

This is a good attempt at writing a detailed and friendly letter. There is fairly good control of language and evidence of range, especially some relevant vocabulary. Errors are non-impeding, for example *Now my country is coming the winter… I'd like to play surffing.*

Band: 4

SAMPLE H (Test 3, Question 8: Letter to a friend)

Hello Thomas, I was very glad when I recieved your letters from Australia. I haven't heard from you for a long time. How are you? Did you find a new job? How are you getting on? At home in Hungary there is nothing specially. I'm sure the whether better there than here. Two weeks before was snowing and the life is stopped. This was the first time where was snowing. At the moment there is no snow inlead always raining. Therfore we can't do any outdoor activities. Only indoors. For example we can go to swim in the swiming pool or play squash in the fitness center. But do you now I every day go to airobic, of course in week days. I hope you can do more outdoors activities. It's more healthy.
Sorry, but I have to finish my letter I promise the next time I'll write more.

Your friend, Jud

Examiner Comments

This is an adequate attempt, showing some control of language. Simple sentence structure is sound, although there are a number of mostly non-impeding errors, for example *I'm sure the whether better there than here... But do you now I every day go to airobic...* The answer requires some effort by the reader.

Band: 3

SAMPLE I (Test 3, Question 8: Letter to a friend)

> *Whats's the weather hir? Rain, rain, rain!*
> *Every morning when I wake up see the same!*
> *I love sun but....*
> *I don't know what write to you about activities which I'm going to do outdoor? When is weather like now I need only sleep! When I get up in the morning I think only about when I come bek to my bed! What you thin about it? Mayby I have go to the doctor?*

Examiner Comments

This is an inadequate attempt, which is slightly short at 76 words and has no opening or closing formulae. There are some non-impeding errors in word order, question formation, use of articles and spelling, for example *When is weather like now... What you thin about it? Mayby I have go to the doctor?*

Band: 2

PAPER 2   LISTENING

Part 1

1 B   2 C   3 C   4 B   5 A   6 A   7 A

Part 2

8 C   9 B   10 A   11 C   12 B   13 C

Part 3

14   (0)7.45
15   sleeping bag / sleep bag
16   swimming / swim
17   drink(s)
18   Post Office
19   (college) entrance hall

Part 4

20 A   21 B   22 A   23 B   24 B   25 B

Test 3 transcript

This is the Cambridge Preliminary English Test number 3. There are four parts to the test. You will hear each part twice.

For each part of the test, there will be time for you to look through the questions and time for you to check your answers.

Write your answers on the question paper. You will have six minutes at the end of the test to copy your answers onto the answer sheet.

The recording will now be stopped. Please ask any questions now, because you must not speak during the test.

[pause]

Now open your question paper and look at Part 1.

[pause]

PART 1   *There are seven questions in this part. For each question there are three pictures and a short recording. Choose the correct picture and put a tick in the box below it.*

Before we start, here is an example.

What's the time?

Woman: Have you got the time?
Man: Yes, it's twenty past three.

[pause]

The first picture is correct so there is a tick in box A.

Look at the three pictures for Question 1 now.

[pause]

Now we are ready to start. Listen carefully. You will hear each recording twice.

One. What is the man going to buy?

Woman: Is everything ready for the holiday?

Man: I'm just going shopping – I must get those pills I take when I feel travel sick. Do we need anything else at the chemist's? We forgot the toothpaste last time!

Woman: I've got that. I haven't got any sunglasses, but I can borrow yours, can't I? And I'll get something to read at the airport.

Man: Right.

[pause]

Now listen again.

[The recording is repeated.]

[pause]

Two. Which dress is Kate talking about?

Girl: Oh Mum, this dress is still dirty!

Woman: It can't be, Kate – I've only just washed it.

Girl: Well it is. The mark on the collar has gone, but there's still a small one here – look it's at the front just below the button. It's where I spilt some Coke last week.

[pause]

Now listen again.

[The recording is repeated.]

[pause]

Three. When will Jane meet them?

Man: Hi, it's Pete here. Jane left a message to say she can't meet us at 8.00 as planned, because her bus doesn't get in till 8.15 and it'll take her 30 minutes to get from the centre of town. I told her the table is actually booked for 8.45 so that would be fine and we'll see her then.

[pause]

Now listen again.

[The recording is repeated.]

[pause]

Four. Which morning activity is for beginners?

Man: At 10.00 a.m. tomorrow morning there will be swimming lessons, at both intermediate and beginner level. Then there will be volleyball practice at 11.30 for all those of you who are already in one of the teams. Also in the morning, for those of you who already know how to sail, there's a chance to do some practice on your own. There will be lessons in both sailing and windsurfing for beginners after lunch.

[pause]

Now listen again.

[The recording is repeated.]

[pause]

Five. Which painting does the woman decide to buy?

Woman: They're all nice, but you see a lot of flowers everywhere these days, don't you, so that wouldn't be my choice. The same goes for animals actually, although I do quite like the one of the horses. So, it looks like it'll have to be the one with the boats. It will be a change from that bowl of fruit I've had on the wall all these years, anyway.

[pause]

Now listen again.

[The recording is repeated.]

[pause]

Six. What is the man selling?

Man: And this is the latest model by Macpoint. You'll find it's even quicker at doing your washing up and needs less water. And it's very easy to use – as easy as turning on your shower.

[pause]

Now listen again.

[The recording is repeated.]

[pause]

Seven. What is the weather forecast for tomorrow?

Woman: … it's been typical spring weather today, sunshine and showers. The next twenty-four hours should be dry but cloudy … Things look better for the next week, with Monday being a fine sunny day and the following day mild but windy …

[pause]

Now listen again.

[The recording is repeated.]

[pause]

That is the end of Part 1.

[pause]

PART 2   *Now turn to Part 2, questions 8–13.*

You will hear a radio presenter talking about new books.
For each question, put a tick in the correct box. You now have 45 seconds to look at the questions for Part 2.

[pause]

Now we are ready to start. Listen carefully. You will hear the recording twice.

Woman: Welcome to this week's book programme. We've got lots of great new books to tell you about.
    My life, by Joe Wrigley, will keep all fans of Joe's stories happy for hours. It explains a lot about where his ideas come from and gives a picture of what was happening in his life when he was working on his most successful books. I must say, though, that some of it is difficult to understand if you haven't read his other books.

Now, for those of you who like a good cry, *Goodbye to the fields*, by Susan Marks, tells the sad story of John, a small boy who has to leave the countryside he loves when the family move to London because of his father's job. John and his mother would prefer to stay where they are. It's a long time before the family begins to feel comfortable living in the big city.

There are plenty of books with helpful advice this week. First, the *A–Z of photography* would make a great present for anyone just starting out with a camera. It has everything you need to know to take really good photos, and learn about cameras, film, lighting and so on. This is not one for the experienced photographer, though – there's not much advanced information here.

Turning to the kitchen, *Cooking for one*, by Adrian White, says on its cover that even people who hate cooking will find it useful. A month ago, I couldn't even boil an egg, but now I'm producing all sorts of dishes, some quite difficult, and, yes, they taste quite good, too. I'm actually enjoying cooking now. I'm now going to try a new book about cooking Italian food.

The last book this week is *Holidays in Europe*, by Mary Curtis. This is an enjoyable read, which will start your imagination working as you plan for next year's holiday. It doesn't matter that the writer doesn't talk about the famous places everyone visits, but describes lots of small places away from the main tourist areas. The maps are too small to be useful but the book is still good value for money.

That's it for this week, then. Next week, there's a special report on giving books as presents, so if you've saved up your money and you're wondering what to get for a friend or relation for their birthdays, you might get some good ideas … I'll look forward to talking to you then …

[pause]

Now listen again.

[The recording is repeated.]

That is the end of Part 2.

[pause]

PART 3   *Now turn to Part 3, questions 14–19.*

You will hear a teacher talking about a camping trip.
For each question, fill in the missing information in the numbered space. You now have 20 seconds to look at Part 3.

[pause]

Now we are ready to start. Listen carefully. You will hear the recording twice.

Man: Thank you all for coming. I'm going to give you the final details of our camping trip next week. You may like to make some notes as there's a lot to remember.

There's a lot to remember.

The coach will be outside the school on Monday morning at 7.30 and we will set off at 7.45 so don't be late. There'll be room on the coach for one bag each so please don't bring more than one bag or suitcase. You don't need to bring tents or food as that's all provided for us, but you will need to bring a sleeping bag. It turns cold at night so bring some warm clothes too. If we're lucky though, the sun will shine and we'll be able to use the outdoor pool on the site so don't forget your swimming things.

On to pocket money – please don't bring too much. We can't keep a lot of money safe. £5 per day should be plenty so you can buy souvenirs and drinks while we are out visiting places.

You will probably also want to bring some extra money for the last day when you are free. The campsite is in the middle of the countryside so if you've had enough fresh air by then, you may want to go shopping in the nearest town about eight miles away. That's Southport. There's plenty to do there and there's a bus that stops outside the Post Office in the village down the road. I'll point it out to you when we get there.

On Friday afternoon, before you leave college, please look at the notice board in the entrance hall as there may be some changes to the arrangements which I need to tell you about.

Now, has anyone got any questions?

[pause]

Now listen again.

[The recording is repeated.]

That is the end of Part 3.

[pause]

PART 4   *Now turn to Part 4, questions 20–25.*

Look at the six sentences for this part. You will hear a conversation between a girl, Lisa, and a boy, Ben, about holidays.
Decide if each sentence is correct or incorrect. If it is correct, put a tick in the box under A for YES. If it is not correct, put a tick in the box under B for NO. You now have 20 seconds to look at the questions for Part 4.

[pause]

Now we are ready to start. Listen carefully. You will hear the recording twice.

Girl: Hi, Ben! Only one more week at college, and then the summer holidays begin. Great, isn't it!

Boy: I don't know. It might get a bit boring. I don't think I've got enough money to go anywhere nice for a holiday this year.

Girl: It <u>would</u> be nice to have lots of money to spend but a good holiday doesn't have to be expensive!

Boy: Oh yes it does! The best holiday I ever had was a few years ago when I went to Greece. I want to fly off somewhere hot, and lie on the beach and go swimming.

Girl: Yes, well, I can't afford to do that, either.

Boy: So what are you doing this summer?

Girl: I'm going on a walking holiday in Scotland with some friends. We went last year, and we really enjoyed it. We walked all day and spent the nights in Youth Hostels. Why don't you come with us? We're going for two weeks. It won't cost much, and you'll come home feeling really relaxed and fit.

Boy: I'm not sure. Walking all day sounds like hard work to me. And surely you're not hoping for lots of sunshine in Scotland?

Girl: It did rain a bit last year, but most of the time it was sunny. Anyway, it's not good walking in the heat. You have to stop all the time to rest and have drinks.

Boy: Well, <u>I</u> like the sun, and I like to stay in comfortable hotels, not Youth Hostels!

Girl: But they <u>are</u> comfortable. They're basic, and the food's often not very good, but they're very clean and cheap. In fact I prefer them to hotels because the people are always so friendly.

Boy: Maybe. Look Lisa, thanks a lot for asking me, but I think I'll just stay home and get bored!

[pause]

Now listen again.

[The recording is repeated.]

That is the end of Part 4.

[pause]

You now have six minutes to check and copy your answers onto the answer sheet.

Note: Teacher, stop the recording here and time six minutes. Remind students when there is **one** minute remaining.

That is the end of the test.

Test 4

PAPER 1   READING AND WRITING

READING

Part 1

1 C   2 A   3 B   4 C   5 B

Part 2

6 C   7 E   8 D   9 H   10 B

Part 3

11 A   12 B   13 B   14 B   15 A   16 A   17 B
18 A   19 B   20 A

Part 4

21 B   22 C   23 A   24 B   25 D

Part 5

26 A   27 B   28 C   29 D   30 B   31 B   32 D
33 C   34 A   35 A

WRITING

Part 1

1 We had a map but it was difficult to find the zoo.

Although we had a map, we	couldn't / could not / didn't / did not	**find the zoo easily.**

2 The car park was outside the main entrance.

There was somewhere	to park	**outside the main entrance.**

3 We wore sun hats because it was very hot.

It was	so (very) hot/sunny	**that we wore sun hats.**

4 Maria suggested going to see the monkeys.

Maria said, 'Why don't we	go to/and see	**the monkeys?'**

5 The elephants were my favourite animals.

I liked the elephants	more/better than	any other animal.

Part 2

The task-specific Mark scheme given below should be used in conjunction with the General Mark scheme for **Writing Part 2** given on page 13.

Task-specific Mark scheme

The content elements that need to be covered are:

i   a suggestion for which hotel your friend should book
ii an explanation of why you are recommending the hotel
iii a suggestion as to what they could do near the hotel

The following sample answers can be used as a guide when marking.

SAMPLE A (Test 4, Question 6: Email to friends)

> Dear friends
>   Before you are going to visit my country, you'd book the most famous hotel of my country, because the hotel has nice food, view and many famous places near by the hotel. By the way, the hotel is nearly my house, so I think you'd book the hotel. I hope to see you soon
>
> Love from
> Hao

Examiner Comments

This is an inadequate attempt, which fails to name the hotel and barely addresses the final point, as no suggestion is made. The writer's friends could make little practical use of the email.

Band: 2

SAMPLE B (Test 4, Question 6: Email to friends)

Hello Sean,

I am very happy because you and Ronan are coming to Mexico, I think that to stay in the Royal Palace Hotel is the best option, I recommend that hotel because is in the centre of the city, is quite nice and not very expensive.

If you like to go for a walk and to know about our culture, this hotel is the best, because everything is near.

You can book the hotel on www.theroyalhotel.com.mx.

Love from

Mayra

Examiner Comments

All content elements are covered appropriately and the message is clearly communicated, with minimal errors. At 75 words, the answer is longer than necessary but has not been penalised, as all the information is relevant to the readers. However, candidates should be trained to observe the word limits.

Band: 5

SAMPLE C (Test 4, Question 6: Email to friends)

> You should book the Ebisu-garden Hotel. Because you can get anywhere easilier from Ebisu.
>
> The Ebisu-garden Hotel was built about five years ago. It has a lot of new things there. It is popular in famous people. A lots of famous people from over the world have been stayed there.

Examiner Comments

In this script, the first two content elements are covered appropriately, but the third element has been omitted. The script can only receive 3, therefore. Language errors do not affect the clarity of the message.

Band: 3

Part 3

The following sample answers and commentaries should be read in conjunction with the General Mark scheme for **Writing Part 3** given on pages 14–15.

SAMPLE D (Test 4, Question 7: The empty house)

> *The empty house*
>
> *That history began when one day a woman who lived in a very big house in Oxford had to move to another city. So she was taking off her furniture from the house during three days, but the last day she fell down the stairs and she died so the house was along and never nobody was to live at this home. Some times some neighbours went at that house but they said that they could see the house with all the furniture in the same place, but when they went at night the woman apeaieced taking off the furniture and the house was empty, the chldren thought it was the woman's phanto.*

Examiner Comments

This is a good attempt at a story, which is well organised and shows some range of structures and vocabulary (the first sentence is particularly good). There is fairly good control, though some non-impeding errors occur as a result of ambition, for example *…she was taking off her furniture.*

Band: 4

SAMPLE E (Test 4, Question 7: The empty house)

When I stay in my home, I remember the teacher told me "You need to do your English homework", so when I starded to do my homework while I was listening footstops, I'm very afraid and in that moment I'm call the police, and the police ask me "what happend are you ok and I said, please come and help me because I'm alone in my house and I think one person try to kill me.

In that moment I'm very scared and then I don't remember anything, when I woke up this morning all things are ok, but I don't have to do my homework, so I think the teacher's never have do English homework because every time something is wrong.

Examiner Comments

Although the candidate has tried hard to produce a story, the numerous errors make it difficult to follow and require considerable effort by the reader. Past tenses are problematic, for example *I'm call the police, and the police ask me "what happend…"*.

Band: 2

SAMPLE F (Test 4, Question 7: The empty house)

> The empty house
> One day when I got home I didn't find anything, unfurtinatly my house was stolen. It is thought that the robe was made at Mid-day when I was out, However some neighbours of mine saw the people that made it. Now the police is investigating the clues and I have to wait for the answer.
> I was very sad because sadenly somebody robe your things which you had got with hours of hard work and now you have to start again.
> Is life!!!
> What I mean is please be carefull with your owns things because always someone is waiting to robe you.

Examiner Comments

This answer contains a number of non-impeding errors but at the same time, there is some range of language, such as *investigating the clues...* and some control of more complex sentences, for example *However some neighbours of mine saw the people that ...*. The candidate has problems with the commonly confused words *do/make* and *rob/burgle/steal*.

Band: 3

SAMPLE G (Test 4, Question 8: Letter to a friend)

Dear Friend

I think, if you looking for a part-time job is very good option, I think the best place is in a café because you meet a lot of people and you received more money and the job is very hard but in my opion is a good job.

You need think about what do you want? And of course wich place do you like more. If you acepted the job it's very good because you have your own money and you no't necesary dependent of your parent.

I hope you choice the best option and enjoy this job.

With love

Vanessa Candioti

Examiner Comments

This is a borderline Band 2/3 script but the numerous errors, particularly in tense formation and the spelling of PET-level words, place it in Band 2, for example *If you looking for... in my opion... . I hope you choice...* . The candidate also has problems with modal verbs, for example *You need think about...* . The organisation of the letter is quite good and with better control, the candidate would have scored a higher mark.

Band: 2

SAMPLE H (Test 4, Question 8: Letter to a friend)

Hello,

I have recieved your letter and knowed you are going to find a job if I were you I would get a job in the café than a shop following two reasons.

Firstly, in the café the etomosphere is more friendly than shop because most of people who go to café just want to relax and they almost very happy. So you can easy to talk with them and make even friends with them.

Secondly you can work in the café in the night and avoid have impact with your course. After study hard in the daytime you can relax in the café and also can get money. I think it's fit for you who don't stay at home in the night.

Ok, that is my advice for you but decide by yourself. Hope you can find a good part-time job.

Examiner Comments

This answer is ambitious and fluent, showing some range of structures and vocabulary, such as *if I were you I would get... .* However, it is flawed by a number of mainly non-impeding errors, for example *the etomosphere is more friendly than shop... After study hard in the daytime... .*

Band: 3

SAMPLE I (Test 4, Question 8: Letter to a friend)

Dear Hazel

I want to tell you something, if you want fun, you have to look for a job in a café because in cafes always there are a lot of young people and sometimes they are looking for new friends and you can meet new people every weekend. This is my advice, I think that if you get a job in a café, you will be very happy.

Another good thing about working in a café is the money, you will earn more money in a café than in a shop.

I hope you are fine and I am sure, you will make the best deccission and you will do very well.

I love you

Mayra

Examiner Comments

The candidate has produced a competent and friendly letter. There is generally good control and effective linking, for example *Another good thing about working in a café…* . Errors are minor and occur mainly in spelling. The answer would receive a low Band 5 mark, due to the absence of vocabulary range.

Band: 5

Key

Part 1

1 B   2 B   3 C   4 A   5 C   6 B   7 C

Part 2

8 C   9 C   10 B   11 A   12 A   13 B

Part 3

14 cakes
15 (fresh) fish
16 vegetables
17 15/fifteen minutes
18 Canada
19 23 March

Part 4

20 B   21 B   22 A   23 B   24 B   25 A

Test 4 transcript

This is the Cambridge Preliminary English Test number 4. There are four parts to the test. You will hear each part twice.

For each part of the test, there will be time for you to look through the questions and time for you to check your answers.

Write your answers on the question paper. You will have six minutes at the end of the test to copy your answers onto the answer sheet.

The recording will now be stopped. Please ask any questions now, because you must not speak during the test.

[pause]

Now open your question paper and look at Part 1.

[pause]

PART 1   *There are seven questions in this part. For each question there are three pictures and a short recording. Choose the correct picture and put a tick in the box below it.*

Before we start, here is an example.

Where did the man leave his camera?

Man: Oh no! I haven't got my camera!
Woman: But you used it just now to take a photograph of the fountain.
Man: Oh I remember, I put it down on the steps while I put my coat on.
Woman: Well, let's drive back quickly – it might still be there.

[pause]

The first picture is correct so there is a tick in box A.

Look at the three pictures for Question 1 now.

[pause]

Now we are ready to start. Listen carefully. You will hear each recording twice.

One. Where will the woman go first after work?

Man: Are you and Sarah going straight to the restaurant from work tonight?

Woman: Actually, I'm leaving work early because I need to do some shopping in the market, and I'm going to meet Sarah after that outside the cinema. She doesn't know where the restaurant is, you see. You're playing tennis after work, aren't you?

Man: Yes. So I'll see you at the restaurant.

[pause]

Now listen again.

[The recording is repeated.]

[pause]

Two. What can festival visitors see every day?

Woman: The Arts Centre in London is holding a festival of Irish culture from the 4th to 12th of April. An exhibition of paintings is open daily and on some weekday evenings the Theatre has special events including plays and films. At the weekend, concerts of Irish music will take place in the Town Hall.

[pause]

Now listen again.

[The recording is repeated.]

[pause]

Three. What souvenir will the boy's mother bring?

Woman: What colour T-shirt shall I bring you from New York, Fred?

Boy: I'd prefer black but … actually a baseball cap would be a good idea.

Woman: Mmm. Or what about another model car for your collection? I could get you a New York taxi.

Boy: Great. I really liked the sports car you bought me last time.

[pause]

Now listen again.

[The recording is repeated.]

[pause]

Four. What time is the woman's hair appointment?

Woman 1: I'd like to make an appointment to have my hair cut please. This Friday or Saturday in the morning if you can manage it.

Woman 2: Let me see … we can do Friday at 10.00 or 11.30, then on Saturday there's 9.30 or 12 o'clock.

Woman 1: I'll take the earlier one on Saturday please.

[pause]

Now listen again.

[The recording is repeated.]

[pause]

Five. Where's the TV guide?

Woman: Have you seen the TV guide?

Boy: Isn't it on top of the television? I had it when I was watching the film last night.

Woman: I expect you left it by your chair then. Here it is under the cushion where nobody can find it. You should put it back in its place by the telephone. Then we'd all know where it is.

[pause]

Now listen again.

[The recording is repeated.]

[pause]

Six. What does the man decide to take Tracy?

Man: I'm going to see Tracy in hospital, but I can't think of what to take her. People always take flowers …

Woman: … so she'll have lots already for sure. I always think it's nice to have something to read myself, but as Tracy's got her walkman with her, what about something to listen to?

Man: What a good idea. It's better than taking sweets, certainly, because I know she's on a special diet while she is in hospital.

[pause]

Now listen again.

[The recording is repeated.]

[pause]

Seven. Which sport has the man just started?

Woman: Hi, how was your holiday?

Man: Great, really good windsurfing and sailing – you know how much I enjoy them. And horse-riding … I really want to go again now I've tried it. And the swimming pool was wonderful too – much warmer than the one I usually swim in … holidays are just too short!

[pause]

Now listen again.

[The recording is repeated.]

[pause]

That is the end of Part 1.

[pause]

PART 2   *Now turn to Part 2, questions 8–13.*

You will hear a man called John Dalin talking about the travel programmes he makes for television.
For each question, put a tick in the correct box. You now have 45 seconds to look at the questions for Part 2.

[pause]

Now we are ready to start. Listen carefully. You will hear the recording twice.

Man: People always ask me why I only travel the hard way! A lot of television travel programmes are about relaxing holidays on the beach, but I've only ever made documentaries about really long trips. The last trip I did was a 50,000-mile journey around the Pacific Ocean, and it took 12 months. But then my very first trip was a 'round the world' journey, and the most difficult one was probably a car journey from the North Pole to the South Pole!

As you can imagine, I've seen a lot of the world! I'm lucky to be in really excellent health, but life is very short and I've done so much travelling that I want a change. Travelling long distances makes you extremely tired, and although it's still a great pleasure for me, I want to do something more relaxing now.

I think my next television series might be made nearer England. There's some really interesting work going on in Wales, where they've just found what remains of a 2,000-year-old town. Or I might do something about farms in France, or even cycling in Holland. There's always something to film if you look hard enough!

But I hope the programmes I've made about the really long trips will encourage other people to get on a plane and have some adventures. Some people seem to be afraid of going to a strange country and perhaps being ill there, but maybe they realise now that if I can do these trips, so can they. I'm only a very ordinary person. And obviously, you don't have to travel on your own as I always have.

I must say that until recently I hadn't ever worried about being so far from home even when the children were very small. But while I was filming in Borneo last year my wife had to have an emergency operation, and it really frightened me because I couldn't get back to England. Everything was fine in the end – but I wouldn't want to be so far away if anything like that happened to my family again.

Perhaps if I spend more time at home I can do more writing. I've done two books so far. I write about places I've seen and my feelings about them. I don't think I'll ever write fiction or poetry, but I'd be interested in writing newspaper articles. My family says I'm very difficult to live with when I'm writing at home … perhaps that's why they've never complained about me travelling!

[pause]

Now listen again.

[The recording is repeated.]

That is the end of Part 2.

[pause]

PART 3   *Now turn to Part 3, questions 14–19.*

You will hear a woman talking on the radio about an exhibition of food and cooking. For each question, fill in the missing information in the numbered space. You now have 20 seconds to look at Part 3.

[pause]

Now we are ready to start. Listen carefully. You will hear the recording twice.

Woman: Today, I want to tell you about the Good Food Show at the Capital Exhibition Centre. There are more than 300 stands at the exhibition. I really enjoyed my visit.

First I looked at the books on sale. Jane Adams, the famous television cook, was there signing copies of her latest book. It's about making cakes so I had to have it! My family loves sweet things and I really liked her last book about making bread. There's a different famous cook there every day signing books and talking to people.

In fact, there's advice on all sorts of topics. I listened to someone from the central market talking about what you should look for when you buy fish. I've always been nervous about buying it, because how can you tell if it's really fresh? Well, I think I've got a better idea now.

Then, in the exhibition theatre, I saw a cook prepare a healthy but tasty lunch using only vegetables! They will prepare a different dish every day. Also in the theatre, at 2 o'clock every day, a cook talks about preparing delicious desserts in under 15 minutes. I tasted one made with chocolate and it was out of this world!

At the show, you can try food from all around the world, from Chile to China, and I did! I enjoyed the food from Canada most of all, although everything I tasted was really good.

The exhibition centre is open from 9 a.m. to 8 p.m. from Monday to Saturday and from 10 until 6 on Sundays. But hurry, because the last day is the 23rd of March when the Good Food Show has to make way for the Boat Show. For more details, phone …

[pause]

Now listen again.

[The recording is repeated.]

That is the end of Part 3.

[pause]

PART 4   *Now turn to Part 4, questions 20–25.*

Look at the six sentences for this part. You will hear a conversation between a teenage girl called Anna and her father about a party.
Decide if each sentence is correct or incorrect. If it is correct, put a tick in the box under A for YES. If it is not correct, put a tick in the box under B for NO. You now have 20 seconds to look at the questions for Part 4.

[pause]

Now we are ready to start. Listen carefully. You will hear the recording twice.

Girl: Are you busy Dad? I've got something I want to ask you. I've been invited to a party on Saturday. Would you give me a lift there?
Man: Where is the party then?
Girl: It's at Tom's house. His sister is 18 on Saturday, and they're having a big celebration. It's going to be brilliant. They're having a disco and Tom's Mum's a wonderful cook, so the food will be good. They've invited all their friends from school but their cousins will be there too.
Man: Well, I hope the weather stays warm so you can be outside. It sounds as if a lot of people are coming. But it all sounds fine to me. It'll be nice for you to go out at the weekend. You spend too much time at home studying. Now, what time does the party start and what time does it finish?
Girl: It starts at eight o'clock and finishes about half past twelve. But Jane's going as well, and <u>her</u> Dad will collect us and bring us home afterwards. It's all arranged.

Man: Mmm … it'll be difficult for us to <u>take</u> you. Mum and I are going to see a film which starts at 7.15. Let's see. Why don't <u>we</u> collect you and Jane at the end of the party? Then you could ask Jane's Dad to <u>take</u> you both to the party at eight.

Girl: I'm sure that'll be fine. I'll go and give Jane a ring.

Man: Just one thing though – we'll pick you up at 11.30. I really think that's late enough.

Girl: Oh Dad! That's so early. Remember we don't have to go to school on Sunday! Don't make us leave an hour before everyone else.

Man: Well, I suppose it <u>is</u> the weekend. Let's say midnight. But definitely <u>no</u> later.

Girl: But …

Man: That's my final decision! Now go and ring Jane before I change my mind!

Girl: Okay.

[pause]

Now listen again.

[The recording is repeated.]

That is the end of Part 4.

[pause]

You now have six minutes to check and copy your answers onto the answer sheet.

Note: Teacher, stop the recording here and time six minutes. Remind students when there is **one** minute remaining.

[pause]

That is the end of the test.

Lightning Source UK Ltd.
Milton Keynes UK
UKOW021227110613

212048UK00002B/58/P